First World War
and Army of Occupation
War Diary
France, Belgium and Germany

35 DIVISION
105 Infantry Brigade
Cheshire Regiment
16th Battalion
30 January 1916 - 8 February 1918

WO95/2487/2

The Naval & Military Press Ltd
www.nmarchive.com
Published in association with The National Archives

Published by

The Naval & Military Press Ltd

Unit 10 Ridgewood Industrial Park,

Uckfield, East Sussex,

TN22 5QE England

Tel: +44 (0) 1825 749494

www.naval-military-press.com

www.nmarchive.com

This diary has been reprinted in facsimile from the original. Any imperfections are inevitably reproduced and the quality may fall short of modern type and cartographic standards.

© Crown Copyright
Images reproduced by permission of The National Archives, London, England, 2015.

Contents

Document type	Place/Title	Date From	Date To
Heading	WO95/2487/2 16 Battalion Cheshire Regiment.		
War Diary	Southampton.	30/01/1916	30/01/1916
War Diary	Havre.	31/01/1916	02/02/1916
War Diary	Wollan Cappel	03/02/1916	03/02/1916
War Diary	Molinghem.	09/02/1916	09/02/1916
War Diary	Hamet Billet.	19/02/1916	19/02/1916
War Diary	Les Choquaux.	20/02/1916	20/02/1916
War Diary	Robecq.	29/02/1916	29/02/1916
War Diary	Gorre.	07/03/1916	07/03/1916
War Diary	Givenchy.	10/03/1916	15/03/1916
War Diary	Pacaut.	19/03/1916	21/03/1916
War Diary	Estaires.	25/03/1916	25/03/1916
War Diary	Laventie.	26/03/1916	12/04/1916
War Diary	Sailly.	13/04/1916	13/04/1916
War Diary	Le Croix Marmuse.	18/04/1916	18/04/1916
War Diary	Richebourg St. Vaast.	19/04/1916	19/04/1916
War Diary	Ferme Du Bois.	23/04/1916	27/04/1916
War Diary	Richebourg St. Vaast.	28/04/1916	28/04/1916
Heading	35th Division 105th Infy Bde 16th Bn Cheshire. Regt Jan 1916-Feb 1918 Disbanded.		
War Diary	Richebourg St. Vaast.	01/05/1916	01/05/1916
War Diary	Ferme Du Bois.	03/05/1916	06/05/1916
War Diary	Fosse.	07/05/1916	07/05/1916
War Diary	Neuve Chapelle.	14/05/1916	18/05/1916
War Diary	Croix Barbee.	19/05/1916	19/05/1916
War Diary	Neuve Chapelle.	22/05/1916	27/05/1916
War Diary	Croix Barbee.	28/05/1916	31/05/1916
War Diary	Neuve Chapelle.	01/06/1916	08/06/1916
War Diary	Croix Barbee.	09/06/1916	16/06/1916
War Diary	Fosse.	16/06/1916	16/06/1916
War Diary	Hinges.	17/06/1916	30/06/1916
Heading	105th Bde. 35th Div. War Diary 16th Battalion Cheshire Regiment 1st To 31st July 1916 Report On Operations 18/19th July with 105th Brigade War Diary.		
Miscellaneous	H 62	08/08/1916	08/08/1916
War Diary	Hinges.	01/07/1916	03/07/1916
War Diary	Sus. St. Ledger.	03/07/1916	03/07/1916
War Diary	Beauval.	07/07/1916	07/07/1916
War Diary	Bus-Les Artois.	10/07/1916	10/07/1916
War Diary	Warloy Baillon.	11/07/1916	11/07/1916
War Diary	Heilly.	11/07/1916	11/07/1916
War Diary	Bois Celestines.	12/07/1916	12/07/1916
War Diary	Grove Town.	13/07/1916	13/07/1916
War Diary	Trones Wood.	16/07/1916	16/07/1916
War Diary	Trenches.	19/07/1916	19/07/1916
War Diary	Trones Wood Waterlot Fm.	16/07/1916	19/07/1916
War Diary	Bricquitrie.	19/07/1916	19/07/1916
War Diary	Talus Boise.	20/07/1916	23/07/1916
War Diary	Carnoy.	23/07/1916	23/07/1916
War Diary	Old German Trenches.	24/07/1916	25/07/1916

War Diary	Dublin Trenches.	26/07/1916	28/07/1916
War Diary	Malt Horn Farm Trench.	23/07/1916	30/07/1916
War Diary	Bivouac South Of Carnoy.	30/07/1916	31/07/1916
War Diary	Bivouac Sand Pit Valley.	31/07/1916	02/08/1916
Heading	105th Brigade. 35th Division. 1/16th Battalion Cheshire Regiment August 1916.		
War Diary	Bois Des Tailles.	02/08/1916	05/08/1916
War Diary	Molliens Vidame.	06/08/1916	10/08/1916
War Diary	Citadel.	10/08/1916	20/08/1916
War Diary	Arrow Head Copse	20/08/1916	22/08/1916
War Diary	Silesia Trenches.	22/08/1916	23/08/1916
War Diary	Bronfay Farm.	23/08/1916	26/08/1916
War Diary	Sand Pit Valley.	26/08/1916	28/08/1916
War Diary	Bois Des Tailles.	28/08/1916	30/08/1916
War Diary	Beaumetz.	30/08/1916	31/08/1916
War Diary	Lucheux.	31/08/1916	01/09/1916
War Diary	Agnez Les Duisans.	01/09/1916	02/09/1916
War Diary	Arras.	02/09/1916	30/11/1916
War Diary		23/11/1916	30/11/1916
War Diary		25/11/1916	25/11/1916
War Diary	Arras 1st Duck 3rd.	27/11/1916	03/12/1916
War Diary	Duizans.	05/12/1916	31/12/1916
War Diary		14/12/1916	31/12/1916
War Diary	Duisans.	01/01/1917	31/01/1917
War Diary	Duisans.	02/02/1917	02/02/1917
War Diary	Lattre-St. Quentin.	03/02/1917	03/02/1917
War Diary	Buneville.	06/02/1917	06/02/1917
War Diary	Flesselles.	06/02/1917	18/02/1917
War Diary	Demuin.	19/02/1917	20/02/1917
War Diary	Vrely.	21/02/1917	28/02/1917
War Diary	Camp Des Ballons.	01/03/1917	01/03/1917
War Diary	Chilly Sector.	02/03/1917	06/03/1917
War Diary	Rosieres.	04/03/1917	04/03/1917
War Diary	Camp Des Ballons.	08/03/1917	14/03/1917
War Diary	Chilly Sub Sector.	15/03/1917	18/03/1917
War Diary	Hyencourt.	19/03/1917	25/03/1917
War Diary	Mesnil Le Petit.	25/03/1917	02/04/1917
War Diary	Offoy.	03/04/1917	11/04/1917
Map	New Work In Green.		
War Diary	Offoy.	12/04/1917	12/04/1917
War Diary	Monchy Lagache & Merau Court.	13/04/1917	14/04/1917
War Diary	Villeveque.	15/04/1917	16/04/1917
War Diary	Maissemy.	17/04/1917	20/04/1917
War Diary	Front Line.	21/04/1917	25/04/1917
War Diary	Maissemy.	26/04/1917	30/04/1917
War Diary	Trefcon Ref Map Sheet 62 C. S.E.	01/05/1917	08/05/1917
War Diary	Fresnoy Section Of Line Ref Map Sheet 62 B. S.W.	09/05/1917	11/05/1917
War Diary	Maissemy.	12/05/1917	15/05/1917
War Diary	Fresnoy Section Of Front Line.	16/05/1917	20/05/1917
War Diary	Soyecourt.	20/05/1917	22/05/1917
War Diary	Peronne.	23/05/1917	25/05/1917
War Diary	Templeux La Fosse.	26/05/1917	31/05/1917
War Diary	105 Infantry Brigade.	02/07/1917	02/07/1917
War Diary	Templeux La Fosse.	01/06/1917	11/06/1917
War Diary	Villers Guislain.	11/06/1917	18/06/1917
War Diary	Templeux La Fosse.	19/06/1917	26/06/1917

War Diary	Revelon.	21/06/1917	01/07/1917
War Diary	Villers Faucon.	02/07/1917	06/07/1917
War Diary	Kildare Post-Epehy Sector.	07/07/1917	12/07/1917
War Diary	Kildare Post.	13/07/1917	15/07/1917
War Diary	Aizecourt Le Bas.	16/07/1917	23/07/1917
War Diary	Quarry 62 C NE F.27 C.D.C. Sector Lempire Sector.	24/07/1917	25/07/1917
War Diary	Quarry.	26/07/1917	01/08/1917
War Diary	Templeux La Fosse.	02/08/1917	10/08/1917
War Diary	Lempire.	11/08/1917	22/08/1917
War Diary	St Emelie.	23/08/1917	27/08/1917
War Diary	Templeux La Fosse.	28/08/1917	31/08/1917
War Diary	Aizecourt.	01/09/1917	01/09/1917
War Diary	St Emilie.	02/09/1917	06/09/1917
War Diary	Ken Lane.	07/09/1917	12/10/1917
War Diary	Aizecourt.	13/10/1917	17/10/1917
War Diary	Adelphi.	18/10/1917	21/10/1917
War Diary	Vaughan's Bank.	22/10/1917	25/10/1917
War Diary	The Nest.	26/10/1917	30/10/1917
War Diary	Aizecourt Peronne.	01/10/1917	03/10/1917
War Diary	Wanquentin	04/10/1917	12/10/1917
War Diary	Arneke	13/10/1917	14/10/1917
War Diary	Proven.	15/10/1917	15/10/1917
War Diary	Elverdinghe.	16/06/1917	20/06/1917
War Diary	South Of Houlthurst Forest.	21/10/1917	23/10/1917
War Diary	Elverdinghe.	24/10/1917	29/10/1917
War Diary	Coldstream Camp.	30/10/1917	01/11/1917
War Diary	De Wippe.	02/11/1917	04/11/1917
War Diary	Proven.	05/11/1917	07/11/1917
War Diary	Elverdinghe	08/11/1917	16/11/1917
War Diary	Brake Camp.	17/11/1917	24/11/1917
War Diary	Poelcapelle.	25/11/1917	26/11/1917
War Diary	Kempton Park.	27/11/1917	30/11/1917
Heading	16th Battn Cheshire Regt. War Diary-December, 1917 Vol 23.		
War Diary	Siege Camp.	01/12/1917	05/12/1917
War Diary	Poelcapelle.	06/12/1917	09/12/1917
War Diary	Le Nouveau Monde.	10/12/1917	10/12/1917
War Diary	School Camp.	11/12/1917	31/12/1917
War Diary	School Camp Popperinghe.	01/01/1918	09/01/1918
War Diary	Brigade Camp Elverdinghe.	10/01/1918	15/01/1918
War Diary	Kempton Park.	16/01/1918	19/01/1918
War Diary	Norfolk House Poelcappelle.	20/01/1918	24/01/1918
War Diary	Kempton Park.	25/01/1918	03/02/1918
War Diary	Bridge Junction.	03/02/1918	08/02/1918
War Diary	Merckeghem.	08/02/1918	08/02/1918

WO95/2487/2
16 Battalion Cheshire Regiment

Army Form C. 2118

Copy 8 Vol 1
XXXV N.O. Bar Cheshire Rgt.
105
35

WAR DIARY
INTELLIGENCE SUMMARY
(Erase heading not required.)

Instructions regarding War Diaries and Intelligence Summaries are contained in F.S. Regs., Part II. and the Staff Manual respectively. Title Pages will be prepared in manuscript.

Place	Date	Hour	Summary of Events and Information	Remarks and references to Appendices
SOUTHAMPTON	30-1-16		Embarked for HAVRE, 34 Officers, 984 other ranks. Commanding Officer :- LT. COL. R. BROWNE CLAYTON. Second-in-command :- MAJOR WORTHINGTON. Adjutant CAPTAIN C. JOHNSON. Quarter Master: HON LIEUT. H. HALSALL. Transport Officer: LIEUT. T. HARE. Signalling Officer LIEUT. A.J.C. STYLES. Company Commanders :- CAPT S.C. BACON, MAJOR J.C. BOWE — CAPT G. PLAYFER — CAPT C. STURLA. Second in command of Coys :- CAPT E.F. THURGOOD — CAPT A.H. HURST — CAPT D. BURNETT — LIEUT H.D. RYALLS. Other officers :- LIEUT S.G. HEWITT — W.R. BATTY — J.D. HODGSON — J.R. DOVENER — R.F. LAWRENSON. G. GEARL. 2nd LIEUTS. P.H. JONES — H. HALSALL — S.G. BOWE — L. MILLINGTON — J.A. BLAKE. M.L. ABRAHAMS — R. McLAREN — R.P. HARRISON — W. FINDLAY — J.B. MENNIE. W. WALLACE — R.P. SCHOLEFIELD — R.D. ECCLESTON. MEDICAL OFFICER :- LIEUT. F.N. STEWART, K.A.M.C.	Oct '16 Dec '16 C.J.
HAVRE	31-1-16		Arrived early morning and marched to Rest Camp.	C.J.
HAVRE	4-2-16		Entrained for BLENDECQUE and arrived morning of 3rd FEBRUARY 1916.	C.J.
WOLLAN CAPPELN	3-2-16		Proceeded from BLENDECQUE to WOLLAN CAPPEL, march route, plotix. till 9-2-16.	C.J.
MOLINGHEM	9-2-16		Proceded from WOLLAN CAPPEL to MOLINGHEM, march route, plotix till 19-2-16.	C.J.
HAMET BILLET	19-2-16		Proceeded from MOLINGHEM to HAMET BILLET, marchroute, rested for the night.	C.J.
LES CHOQUAUX	20-2-16		Marched from HAMET BILLET to LES. CHOQUAUX, in reserve to 38th Division till 29-2-16	C.J.
ROBECQ	29-2-16		Marched from LES. CHOQUAUX to ROBECQ, in rest billets till 7-3-16	C.J.
GORRE	7-3-16		Marched to GORRE for attachment to 114th BRIGADE, 38th Division for instruction in Trench Warfare. Companies attached respectively to 10th WELSH RGT — 13th WELSH RGT — 15th WELSH RGT and 16TH WELSH RGT, 7-3-16 to 15-2-16.	C.J. I.K. 2 shts.

Army Form C. 2118

WAR DIARY or INTELLIGENCE SUMMARY

(Erase heading not required.)

1/4th Bn. Cheshire Rgt.

Instructions regarding War Diaries and Intelligence Summaries are contained in F.S. Regs., Part II. and the Staff Manual respectively. Title Pages will be prepared in manuscript.

Place	Date	Hour	Summary of Events and Information	Remarks and references to Appendices
GIVENCHY	10·3·16		Killed No 16/30635 PTE G. E. WILE "W" Coy. mine explosion, buried WINDY CORNER CEMETRY- GIVENCHY. Wounded 2 men	e.J.
— DITTO —	12·3·16		Killed in action No 16/21777 PTE J. MARSH "Z" Coy- No 16/21984 PTE T.J. M⁰CUE, buried WINDY CORNER CEMETRY. Wounded – 6 men (all casualties caused by Rifle Grenades)	e.J.
— DITTO —	13·3·16		Killed No 16/21456 CORPL J ADAMS. Z. Coy. buried WINDY CORNER CEMETRY. GIVENCHY Wounded 4 men (all casualties caused by RIFLE GRENADES.)	e.J.
— DITTO —	15·3·16		Relieved from trenches and proceeded to CALONNE. Relief wiped till 19.3.16	e.J.
PACAUT	19·3·16		Billeted till 25·3·16	e.J.
— DITTO —	21·3·16		One man (No 16/21363 PTE C. REEDER died from wounds, buried BETHUNE	e.J.
ESTAIRES	25·3·16		Marched to ESTAIRES and billeted for the night.	e.J.
LAVENTIE	26·3·16		Marched to LAVENTIE, relieved 2ⁿᵈ WEST YORKS Brigade Reserve LAVENTIE SECTOR	e.J.
— DITTO —	30·3·16		Relieved 15ᵀᴴ BATTⁿ SHERWOOD FORESTERS in front line, relief commenced 8 p.m. Completed 9.30 p.m.	e.J.
— DITTO —	31·3·16		Killed No 16/20677 PTE EASTWOOD 'W' Coy. buried HOUGOUMONT POST Cemetry Three men wounded.	e.J.

31/3/16

E Johnson Capt & Adjutant
1/4 @ Cheshire Regt.

WAR DIARY
INTELLIGENCE SUMMARY
(Erase heading not required.)

16 Cheshire
Army Form C. 2118
XXXV
Vol 3

Place	Date	Hour	Summary of Events and Information	Remarks and references to Appendices
LAVENTIE	1.4.16	6.50pm	Combined "Strafe" organised against enemy front line and communication French Artillery, Trench mortars and grenades to bombard enemy SECTION. machine guns firing at breaches in parapet. The above postponed owing to Brigade on our right flank carrying out relief.	CJ
LAVENTIE	2.4.16		The above minor operations were carried out successfully the result of Artillery bombardment could not be observed owing to dusk & the density of smoke, the enemy replied with machine gun fire along our parapet and put up a barrage of artillery fire along our return line — no casualties	CJ
LAVENTIE	3.4.16		Day passed quietly, the enemy artillery bombarding and setting fire to a house behind our lines, evidently suspected by them of being an observation post, as upon rooms were occupied and a good view of GERMAN LINE could be obtained. one man wounded	CJ
LAVENTIE	4.4.16		Relieved from front line by 15th Bn The Sherwood Foresters, relief completed at 10 pm. Battalion moved into Reserve billets at LAVENTIE.	CJ
LAVENTIE	5.4.16 to 8.4.16		Battalion in Brigade Reserve.	CJ
LAVENTIE	8.4.16		Relieved 15th Bn Sherwood Foresters, relief completed 9-30 pm.	Swindell CJ
LAVENTIE	9.4.16		Day passed fairly quietly	2 K 3 aets CJ

WAR DIARY
or
INTELLIGENCE SUMMARY
(Erase heading not required.)

Army Form C. 2118

Instructions regarding War Diaries and Intelligence Summaries are contained in F.S. Regs., Part II. and the Staff Manual respectively. Title Pages will be prepared in manuscript.

Place	Date	Hour	Summary of Events and Information	Remarks and references to Appendices
LAVENTIE	10/4/16		Minor operations carried out in conjunction with Artillery and Trench mortar batteries. Two men killed; buried at "ROYAL IRISH RIFLES cemetery. (23277 Pte HALLSWORTH and 24672 Pte MARSH-) one man wounded.	C.J.
LAVENTIE	11/4/16		Day passed fairly quiet, enemy artillery shelled RUE TILLELOY. Two men wounded.	C.J.
LAVENTIE	12/4/16		Relieved by 17th (S) Bn Royal Scots; relief completed 10pm without incident. Battalion moved to SAILLY in Divisional Reserve. One man wounded.	C.J.
SAILLY	13/4/16		In reserve till 18/4/16 at SAILLY - billets occupied by Z Company shelled by enemy Artillery 15/4/16, damaged billets but no casualties.	C.J.
LE CROIX MARMUSE	18/4/16		Moved into billets at MARMUSE for night, enroute for FERME DU BOIS sector of line	C.J.
RICHEBOURG ST VAAST	19/4/16		Relieved 9th Cheshires, Battalion in reserve left sub section, relief completed 12·30 p.m. without incident.	C.J.
FERME du BOIS	23/4/16		Relieved 15th Battn Cheshire Regt in left sub section, FERME du BOIS Sector, one man wounded	C.J.
— Do —	24/4/16		Two men wounded	C.J.

Army Form C. 2118

WAR DIARY

INTELLIGENCE SUMMARY

(Erase heading not required.)

Instructions regarding War Diaries and Intelligence Summaries are contained in F.S. Regs, Part II. and the Staff Manual respectively. Title Pages will be prepared in manuscript.

Place	Date	Hour	Summary of Events and Information	Remarks and references to Appendices
FERME du BOIS.	25/4/16		No 16/29641 Pte. DUCKWORTH. W Coy. Killed, buried at RUE DE BERCEAUX Cemetery RICHEBOURG ST VAAST – one man wounded.	c.J
– Do –	26/4/16		Nothing of incident –	c.J
– Do –	27/4/16		Three artillery operation by the Brigade on our immediate left brought retaliation by GERMAN Artillery, especially on BOARS. HEAD held by W COMPANY – KILLED 21445 CORPL TULL Y Company – 21845 L/Cpl HERMAN Y Coy 20525 Pte. ASHER W Coy, buried RUE DE BERCEAUX Cemetery – WOUNDED: Seventeen men wounded of which two 15/19798 Pte DACY Y Coy and 16/21821 Pte MALPAS died of wounds. Buried at MERVILLE, from No 7 Casualty Clearing Station. – Relieved from front line trenches by 15th (S)Bn The Cheshire Regiment.	c.J
RICHEBOURG ST VAAST	28/4/16		In Brigade Reserve 28/4/16 to 30/4/16 at RICHEBOURG. ST VAAST.	c.J

1-5-16.

C. Johnson Captain Adjutant
16@Bn The Cheshire Regiment

35TH DIVISION
105TH INFY BDE

16TH BN CHESHIRE REGT
JAN ~~FEB~~ 1916 - FEB 1918

DISBANDED

WAR DIARY
or
INTELLIGENCE SUMMARY
(Erase heading not required.)

Army Form C. 2118

XXXV 16. Cheshires VOL 4

Place	Date	Hour	Summary of Events and Information	Remarks and references to Appendices
RICHEBOURG ST VAAST	1-5-16		Battalion in reserve till 2.5.16	CJ
FERME DU BOIS	3.5.16		Relieved 15th (S) Bn Cheshires in front line trenches, relief completed without incident	CJ
— Do —	4.5.16		Nothing of incident to record	CJ
— Do —	5.5.16		Minor operations carried out in conjunction with Artillery and Trench mortars. Object cutting enemy wire – Operations commenced 9.20 p.m. and finished 9.25 p.m. 25 yards of enemy wire and front line parapet completely destroyed, also small portion of enemy second line parapet breached – Japs kept open by fire of machine guns and rifle batteries – Captain G. G. EARLE wounded and two men during enemy retaliation –	CJ
— Do —	6.5.16		Relieved by 17th (S) Batt. West Yorks Regt, relief completed at 10-15 p.m. without incident, Battalion marched to FOSSE.	CJ
FOSSE	7.5.16		Brigade in reserve 7.5.16. to 14-5-16.	CJ
NEUVE CHAPELLE	14.5.16		Relieved 18th (S) Batt. Lancashire Fusiliers in front line trenches NEUVE CHAPELLE, relief completed without incident 10-15 p.m.	CJ
— Do —	15.5.16		Disposition of Companies. Y Coy right company, X Coy centre Coy, Z Coy left Coy, W Coy in support, holding B Line, CHATEAU POST, CHURCH POST and CURZON POST	CJ
— Do —	16.5.16		Nothing of incident to record	CJ

WAR DIARY

Army Form C. 2118

Instructions regarding War Diaries and Intelligence Summaries are contained in F. S. Regs., Part II. and the Staff Manual respectively. Title Pages will be prepared in manuscript.

INTELLIGENCE SUMMARY

(Erase heading not required.)

Place	Date	Hour	Summary of Events and Information	Remarks and references to Appendices
NEUVE CHAPELLE	17.5.16		One man wounded, artillery, both our own and enemy very active, no damage done by enemy artillery.	CJ
—Do—	18.5.16		Relieved by 1st Bn. Cheshire Regiment – relief completed without incident at 11.15 p.m.	CJ HoR
CROIX BARBEE	19.5.16		Battalion in Reserve until 22.5.16. Enemy shelled Billets at intervals each day. 5 men wounded. HoR	
NEUVE CHAPELLE	22.5.16		Relieved 1st Bn Cheshire Regiment – relief completed without incident at 11.5 p.m. W Company right Coy – X Coy centre, Z Coy Left Company, Y Coy in Support. Killing Blanc – CHATEAU POST – CURZON POST – NOR CHURCH POST.	HoR
—Do—	23.5.16		Artillery active on both sides active – 1 man wounded.	HoR
—Do—	24.5.16		Artillery again active on both sides. 2 men wounded. At 10.30 p.m. Artillery is engaged with T.M.s fuel on POPES NOSE in Right Battalion's frontage. Enemy retaliated on our front line at B Wire. HoR	
—Do—	25.5.16		Nothing of interest to report. Capt S.C. Bacon wounded – 1 O.R. killed and 3 men wounded. HoR	
—Do—	26.5.16		At 11 p.m. Artillery is engaged with T.M.s fuel as enemy prepared wire at S.5.b.45.15. Artillery also barraged enemy second line and C.T.s, at night at left of S.5.b.45.15. At 11.10 T.M.s ceased fire. Party of 7 officers and 96 O.R. advanced with the object of raiding enemy's front line at S.5.b. 45.15. At 11.13 p.m. artillery lifted. Raiding party divided into attack and covering parties – knel, owing to men of covering party losing direction in the night. Raiding party found enemy's wire passable till being unsupported, did not enter enemy line but threw bombs into his trenches. They then withdrew its while party eventually reaching our front without Casualties. Commencing at 11-7 p.m. enemy artillery barraged a disused hard behind our front line, also firing a few shells without recognition N	Scheme attached.

Army Form C. 2118

WAR DIARY
~~INTELLIGENCE SUMMARY~~
(Erase heading not required.)

Instructions regarding War Diaries and Intelligence Summaries are contained in F.S. Regs., Part II. and the Staff Manual respectively. Title Pages will be prepared in manuscript.

Place	Date	Hour	Summary of Events and Information	Remarks and references to Appendices
NEUVE CHAPELLE	28.5.16		(Cont) effect on our firing line. There was no enemy Machine Gun or rifle retaliation. No casualties. At 11:30 p.m. when the Railway party returned, Companies & Machine Guns opened rapid — there was no retaliation. Our Machine guns fired periodically during the night in S.5.b.4.5.15. H&H	
— Do —	29.5.16		Our Machine guns and Artillery fired periodically on enemy hidden wire and damaged parapet at S.5.b.4.5.15. Enemy retaliated with shrapnel on our front line. Wounded 1 O.R. Relieved by 15th Battalion Cheshire Regiment. Relief completed without incident at 11·5 p.m. H&H	C.J.
CROIX BARBÉE	29.5.16		Battalion in reserve till 31/5/16	C.J.
CROIX BARBÉE	30.5.16		Enemy attacked front line trenches. Tactical progress report attached. One man wounded.	C.J.
CROIX BARBÉE	31.5.16		Relieved 15th (S) Bn Cheshire Regt, dispositions as for 22-5-16 except Y Coy and X Coy exchange positions — X Coy in Support, Y Coy Centre Coy in front line — Relief completed without incident 11-10 p.m.	C.J.

1/6/16.

C Johnson Captain & Adjt
1 6 (S) Bn The Cheshire Regt

June
16 Cheshires
Vol 5
XXXV

Army Form C. 2118

WAR DIARY
or
INTELLIGENCE SUMMARY
(Erase heading not required.)

Place	Date	Hour	Summary of Events and Information	Remarks and references to Appendices
NEUVE CHAPELLE	1.6.16		Nothing of importance to report. A Company 2/8 Worcester Regt and Battalion Head quarters attached to Battn for instruction	CJ
—DITTO—	2.6.16		Day normal	CJ
—DITTO—	3.6.16		Normal. One man killed 2/8 Worcester Regt, one wounded Worcester	CJ
—DITTO—	4.6.16		Enemy artillery bombarded. N.E.B. garrisoned by "W" Company, but parapet breached but quickly rebuilt — one man 2/8 Worcester Regt wounded	CJ
—DITTO—	5.6.16		Enemy artillery shelled front line trenches, nine men wounded one of whom died of wounds No 16/21329 Pte. CORRIGAN. Y Company	CJ
—DITTO—	6.6.16		Day normal :- LIEUT W R BATTY evacuated sick, suspected Enteric Fever	CJ
—DITTO—	7.6.16		Day normal except for enemy artillery who again breached our parapet in two places and kept same open all night time with machine gun fire — Breach repaired by 11am	CJ
—DITTO—	8.6.16		Relieved from front line trenches by 15th Bn Cheshire Regt, complete at 5.30pm without incident, Battalion returned to Brigade Reserve at CROIX BARBEE	CJ
CROIX BARBEE	9.6.16 to 15.6.16		Battalion in Brigade Reserve at CROIX BARBEE till 16/6/16, nothing of importance to report	CJ
FOSSE	16.6.16		Marched to FOSSE and billets for the night, slight gas about 2 am morning of 17th. No casualties	

Army Form C. 2118

WAR DIARY
or
INTELLIGENCE SUMMARY
(Erase heading not required.)

Instructions regarding War Diaries and Intelligence Summaries are contained in F.S. Regs., Part II. and the Staff Manual respectively. Title Pages will be prepared in manuscript.

Place	Date	Hour	Summary of Events and Information	Remarks and references to Appendices
HINGES	17.6.16		Battalion with remainder of Division placed in CORPS RESERVE, Battalion billeted at HINGES.	CJ
HINGES	23.6.16		Battalion attended Brigade Parade for inspection by Genl. Sir. C. MUNRO, G.O.C. 1ST ARMY at CHOCQUES.	CJ
HINGES	28.6.16		All baggage and transport ordered to proceed to BAILLEUL, AUX, CORNAILLES- and Division placed under orders to reinforce 3rd Army.	CJ
HINGES	30.6.16		Battalion still in Corps reserve – Weekly medical report attached.	CJ

C Johnson Captain & Adjt
10(S) Balkeshire Regt.

1875 Wt. W593/826 1,000,000 4/15 J.B.C. & A. A.D.S.S./Forms/C. 2118.

105th Bde.
35th Div.

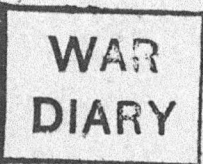

16th BATTALION

CHESHIRE REGIMENT

1st to 31st JULY 1916

Report on Operations 18/19th July with 105th
Brigade War Diary.

105   H 62

Herewith [diary] for July –
The delay in forwarding it
is regretted –

            R Browne Clayton Lt Col
            16th Cheshire Regt

8/8/16

            II
           35 Div

        Forwarded

8/8/16.   Gladstone Capt
                    Bde Mjr
              for GOC 105 Inf Bde

B.S. Tully
Army Form C.2118
July 1916
16 Cheshire

Vol 6

WAR DIARY
or
INTELLIGENCE SUMMARY
(Erase heading not required.)

Instructions regarding War Diaries and Intelligence Summaries are contained in F.S. Regs., Part II and the Staff Manual respectively. Title Pages will be prepared in manuscript.

Place	Date	Hour	Summary of Events and Information	Remarks and references to Appendices
HINGES	1.7.16		In XI Corps reserve till 3.7.16	CJ
HINGES	3.7.16		Entrained at CHOQUES STATION for BOUQUEMAISON and marched to SUS ST LEDGER	CJ
SUS. ST. LEDGER	3.7.16		In billets till 7th July 1916	CJ
BEAUVAL	7.7.16		Marched to BEAUVAL. Transferred from FIRST ARMY to FOURTH ARMY - posted to VIII Corps - billeted in BEAUVAL till 10.7.16	CJ
BUS. les ARTOIS	10.7.16		Marched to BUS. les ARTOIS and camped for the night	CJ
WARLOY BAILLON	11.7.16		Marched to WARLOY BAILLON and billeted	AMc
HEILLY	11.7.16		Marched to HEILLY & camped for the night	AMc
BOIS CELESTINES	12.7.16		Marched to BOIS CELESTINES, rested for three hours & marched by night to bivouac at GROVETOWN south of BRAY	AMc
GROVE TOWN	13/7/16		Marched to BILLON WOOD bivouacced until 16th	AMc
TROMES WOOD	16/7/16		Attached to 54th & 55th Bde marched at 8.40 pm to take up line at TRONES WOOD own line at 5.20 am. A very trying march in heavy rain through very wet communication trench carrying heavy loads	AMc

WAR DIARY or INTELLIGENCE SUMMARY

Army Form C. 2118

Place	Date	Hour	Summary of Events and Information	Remarks and references to Appendices
TRONES WOOD TRENCHES	16/7/16 to 19/7/16		Operations in connection with attack of 2nd line TRONES WOOD WATERLOT FARM. Dispositions Right Company/Field kit in E.D TRONES WOOD from T.24.c.4.1. to T.24.c.2.8. Right Centre Company/from T.24.c.2.8 to the northern extremity of TRONES WOOD - Three companies dug in Trenches into shell holes in front of the wood & connecting these up - Support in deep German dug outs in the wood - Left Centre Company(X) had two platoons in communication Trench at north point of TRONES Wood & T.18.c.3.1. with two platoons in support behind NW corner of TRONES Wood - Left company (W) from T.18.c.3.1. to junction of communication Trenches at T.18.c.6.6. with one platoon in strong point at T.18.c.6.5. Each company had its two Lewis guns, & Mr Vickers guns were disposed along the front - On the morning of the 17th July orders were received from the 54th Bde to take over WATERLOT FM. This Coss'ion was to be done until 12.30 a.m. on the 18th owing to a heavy bombardment by enemy's artillery all along the line - Waterlot Fm was eventually taken over & garrisoned by W company under Lieut Ryalls. Every effort was made to improve & wire the whole line but the only opportunity for wiring was between 5.20 a.m. on the 17th to at midday the same day - at all other times the line was bombarded at the bombardment at times being intense & only short spells of work in the open could be managed. On the morning of the 18th the garrison of WATERLOT FM did excellent work in staying their position - At 2 p.m. the bombardment increased in intensity - at 3/4.hr Lieut Ryalls reports the enemy preparing to attack WATERLOTFM. He reports enemy creeping up the railway embankment from the direction of GUILLEMONT - He sent forward a party with bombs & a Lewis gun to a brick wall which ran parallel to the line of the enemy's advance - Enemy got close under the wall but he bombed them out & turned his Lewis gun on the enemy as they retired down the railway embankment. This was the advance guard to a half of 300 of the enemy with two machine guns which advanced along the Railway embankment - a ricking gun was however placed by Lieut Ryalls & a second took up a position in a shell hole N.E of TRONES WOOD. The Company in WATERLOT FM at the same time opened rifle fire on the advancing enemy. Though the enemy made repeated attempts to work round the S end of WATERLOT FM the cross fire of these two guns & the rifle fire always checked any advance. Enemy casualties up to this point were at least forty - a platoon was sent up to reinforce the	

1875. Wt. W593/826 1,000,000 4/15 J.B.C. & A. A.D.S.S./Forms/C. 2118.

WAR DIARY
or
INTELLIGENCE SUMMARY
(Erase heading not required.)

Army Form C. 2118

Place	Date	Hour	Summary of Events and Information	Remarks and references to Appendices
TRONES WOOD WATERLOT F^m (continues)	16/7/16 to 19/7/16		Garrison of WATERLOT F^m - Artillery support had been unavailable asked for and was obtained at 4.30p.m. The enemy retired leaving however some snipers in field notes who cannot consolidate less until eliminated by the snipers of the garrison - On the N.E. of the farm meanwhile a company of the enemy emerged from DELVILLE WOOD & got into the German trench, making their way in the direction of GUILLEMONT. At the same time the enemy, strong the Battalion minus one of this trench in sun lines & advanced on the farm - 2nd Lieut SCOFIELD who was at the time in command of the two Platoons on the N.E. of the Farm, opened with his Lewis gun & rapid fire at 300 yards range - The enemy who was in very close formation did not retain this fire for long, an officer was seen trying to rally his men, but they eventually retired from behind they had advanced - During this attack 2nd Lieut SCOFIELD was dangerously wounded, & has since died - Serj^t. COOK who took over command of these two platoons estimates the enemy's casualties during this attack at 300, he states that this is if anything an underestimation - There is no doubt the enemy was anxious to find this trench held in such strength, it had been previously known & every endeavour had been made to treat it as a surprise - On the 19th an infantry attack was made by the enemy on WATERLOT F^m, but the whole line held by the Battⁿ was very heavily bombarded during the day, the bombardment was continuous & rendered intense - The trench held by Serj^t COOK was obliterated & rendered untenable - What remained of this garrison with the Lewis gun joined Lieut Ryalls in the trenches S & S.E of the Farm - The Lewis gun was turned three times but recovered & remained in action - The evacuation of this trench exposed Lieut Ryalls left flank, but this was covered as far as possible by a Vickers & Lewis gun in the strong point west of	

WAR DIARY or INTELLIGENCE SUMMARY

Army Form C. 2118

Place	Date	Hour	Summary of Events and Information	Remarks and references to Appendices
TRONES WOOD WATERLOT Fm	19/7/16 to 19/7/16		Waterlot Fm. - The Farm was handed over to the 14th Gloster on the night of 19th/20th July. At 8.30 p.m. on the 19th July a patrol reported the enemy advancing from GUILLEMONT on TRONES Wood. An officers patrol was sent out to confirm this, but he reported no advance on the part of the enemy - We had meanwhile been sent to the Gloster who were on their way to take over the trenches & on the arrival of two of their companies in support I withdrew Coy very slowly holding. Our artillery had at this time opened a heavy fire on the enemy's trenches north of GUILLEMONT which probably stopped any intended attack. The following casualties occurred during these operations. Officers killed: Lieut. A C STYLES. Officers Wounded: 2nd Lieut. A McLAREN (since dead), 2nd Lieut. R P SCOFIELD (since dead), 2nd Lieut. W H FINDLAY, Capt & Adjt C JOHNSON, Lieut Col R BROWNE-CLAYTON, Major R WORTHINGTON, Lieut H D RYALLS & 2 Lieut J A BLAKE. Lieut Col Browne Clayton, Major Worthington & Lieut Ryalls were however slightly wounded & remained at duty. Other Ranks Killed Battn Sergt Major GILES and 31 N.C.O's & men. Wounded 175. Wounded (at duty) 4. Missing 7. Shell shock 5. Accidentally injured 1. Total Killed 33, Wounded 179, Wounded at duty 18, Missing 7, Shellshock 5, Accidentally injured 1, Sick 1. Total all ranks 244. AM

Army Form C. 2118

WAR DIARY
or
INTELLIGENCE SUMMARY
(Erase heading not required.)

Instructions regarding War Diaries and Intelligence Summaries are contained in F. S. Regs., Part II. and the Staff Manual respectively. Title Pages will be prepared in manuscript.

Place	Date	Hour	Summary of Events and Information	Remarks and references to Appendices
BRIQUETRIE	19.7.16	midnight	18 Battn H.Q. at BRIQUETRIE. Batts holding BERNAFAY WOOD trenches. These trenches were shelled during the day. Lieut TANGUY wounded. Battn was relieved during the night & marched to Bivouac at TALUS BOISE	RM
TALUS BOISE	20.7.16 to 23.7.16		Bivouac was shelled at intervals during the day & night. Ten men wounded, Sergt WALSHE included in above subsequently died.	RM
CARNOY	23.7.16		Arrived in bivouac at 9 p.m. Batts marched without transport to MONTAUBAN. Lieut ABRAHAMS wounded accidentally by explosion of bombs belonging to the 14th Gordons.	RM
OLD GERMAN TRENCHES	24.7.16 25.7.16		Trenches shelled occasionally. Two men killed. Seven wounded. One missing.	RM
DUBLIN TRENCHES	26.7.16 to 28.7.16		Took over DUBLIN TRENCHES at 11 a.m. One man accidentally wounded. Two men wounded. On the 28th five men wounded.	RM
MALT HORN FARM TRENCH	28/7/16 to 30/7/16		Took over these trenches just before midnight. The taking over was considerably delayed owing to heavy bombardment. Strength of Battalion holding these trenches 804 all ranks. Trenches bombarded at intervals during the day. Handed over trenches to 30th Division, relief completed at 4.45 a.m. Two men killed. Twelve wounded. One Officer - Batts marched by companies to bivouac Sof CARNOY. The first two miles under heavy shell fire - a considerable number of men were gassed but all remained at duty.	RM
BIVOUAC SOUTH of CARNOY	30/7/16 to 31/7/16		Marched to Bivouac at SAND PIT VALLEY.	RM
BIVOUAC SAND PIT VALLEY	31/7/16 to 2/8/16		Bivouac.	RM

105th Brigade.
35th Division.

1/16th BATTALION

CHESHIRE REGIMENT

AUGUST 1 9 1 6

Army Form C. 2118

Vol 7

16th (S) Battn. Cheshire Regt.

WAR DIARY or INTELLIGENCE SUMMARY

(Erase heading not required)

Instructions regarding War Diaries and Intelligence Summaries are contained in F.S. Regs., Part II. and the Staff Manual respectively. Title Pages will be prepared in manuscript.

Place	Date	Hour	Summary of Events and Information	Remarks and references to Appendices
BOIS DES TAILLES	2.8.16 to 5.8.16		1st Aug. in Bivouac at Sand pit Valley. Marched to BOIS DES TAILLES 2 P.M. Arrived at 6 P.M. Batt. in huts and bivouac Transport moved at 4 P.M. by Road north to DAOURS. Hence 11½ following day to MOLLIENS VIDAME. Batt. entrained at STEENTOWN 10.30 A.M.; detrained 2.H.30PM. at SAIEUX. Marched 1½ miles to billets at MOLLIEN VIDAME.	
MOLLIENS VIDAME	6.7.16 to 10.8.16		Arrived in billets 2 A.M. 6.8.16. On 11th ensuing days batt. was engaged in intensive training on 11th August. Transport moved by route march to DAOURS on 9th and resumed its following day till arrival of CITADEL. On 10th Batt. marched out of billets at 6 A.M. to HINGEST where entrained for MERICOURT at 10 A.M. Distance eight miles. Arriving at 12 latter place 4 P.M. Batt marched to CITADEL a distance of over miles arrived 7 P.M. Here 110 Batt	
CITADEL	10.8.16		Bivouaced. Batt. engaged on working parties and in intensive training	
ARROW HEAD COPSE	20.8.16 22.8.16		At 7.30 P.M. 20.8.16 Batt. marched to and occupied front line trenches at ARROW HEAD COPSE (S.W. of GUILLEMONT) arriving there and completing relief at 2.30 A.M. 21.8.16. The men were heavily laden & the going was bad owing to trenches being slippery through recent rains. We received a Battalion of NORTH STAFFORDSHIRES. Our Trench strength was but all ranks. Suffered casualties 3 killed 20 wounded. 1 sick 19 suffering from shell shock. Previous Rifling into line batt. had been reinforced by a new draft 1/150 men. These men were found to be much below the standard of the old men both in training and physique, and proved a source of anxiety & all during its stay in the line. Were relieved by 14/5 Batt Gloucesters Regt on 1st morning of 22nd relief complete at Sochot. Batt. marched to SILESIA RESERVE TRENCHES arriving there at 9.15 A.M. Here batt was	
SILESIA TRENCHES	22.7.16 23.7.16		subjected to little or no shelling and men were enabled to rest. — Were relieved by 11th(S) 13th ROYAL SCOTS 7 P.M. & Marched to bivouac at BRONFAY FARM. Taking working parties 208 + 300 strong were sent from SILESIA TRENCH to dig new communication trenches at ARROW HEAD COPSE. They joined remainder of batt. in bivouac 3 A.M. 24.8.16	
BRONFAY FARM	22.8.16 25.8.16		Batt. employed in working parties & engaged in intensive training. Brigade were relieved by 15th Bde & Batt. by 1st Warwicks — Marched to SAND PIT VALLEY at 11 A.M. arriving 12.30 bivouac bivouacs.	
SAND PIT VALLEY	26.8.16 to 25.8.16		Intensive Training resumed — Men more or less rested. Batt Marched to Bois des Tailles at 1 P.M. 28.8.16 arriving there 3 P.M. Here we were lodged in huts until	
Bois des TAILLES	28.8.16 30.8.16		Left Bois des Tailles at 12.30 A.M. 30.9.16 Marched to R. HEILLY arriving 10 A.M. distance 10 miles Road very rough & going very bad owing to heavy rains. Men much exhausted Entrained from CANDAS at 7 A.M. arriving at 12 noon. Thence marched to R. BEAUMETZ	
BEAUMETZ	30.8.16 31.8.16		Batt. Marched from BEAUMETZ at 10 A.M. to LUCHEUX Owning 11 Arrival 5 P.M. distance 10 miles. New draft was inspected by A.d.j.t. General who was not entirely satisfied with the men	
LUCHEUX	31.8.16 1.9.16		Left LUCHEUX at 10 A.M. Name Changed by motor lorries to AGNEZ-LES-DUSANS arriving there 12.15 midday. Men billeted - huts etc. Accommodation very poor.	
AGNEZ-LES-DUISANS 2.9.16			Marched to ARRAS to relieve 110th Bde at 6 P.M. 2.9.16	

1875 Wt. W593/826 1,000,000 4/15 J.B.C. & A. A.D.S.S./Forms/C. 2118.

Army Form C. 2118

WAR DIARY or INTELLIGENCE SUMMARY

(Erase heading not required.)

16th - Bn Cheshire Regiment

VOL 8

SEPTEMBER

Instructions regarding War Diaries and Intelligence Summaries are contained in F. S. Regs., Part II. and the Staff Manual respectively. Title Pages will be prepared in manuscript.

Place	Date	Hour	Summary of Events and Information	Remarks and references to Appendices
ARRAS	2.9.16		Batt. arrived 11pm. billeted in caves for night. Moved to front line trenches E. & N.E. ARRAS at 2pm 3.9.16 to relieve 9th Batt Leicestshire Regt. Relief completed at 5.55 pm. without incident or casualty. Batt. occupied Trenches Sector T1. Trench Strength Officers 25 OR's 661 Casualties 1 Scale 4 or killed 22 OR wounded & repairing	
	3.9.16		This part of line particularly quiet. Trenches in very dilapidated condition & occupied all time in renovating & repairing wiring. Patrols out each night along whole front. Patrols also sent out every night. The enemy shews very little activity except with Trench Mortars with which he is well equipped opposite this Sector. Batt still in line to date.	
	30.9.16		Two drafts of 98 + 35 arrived 12th + 18th + latter ones strength. Weather throughout the period generally very good indeed enabling much useful work to be accomplished.	

Marshall J.K.
2 Lieut

J.Prentice Major
Cmdg. 16th Batt Cheshire Regt.

Army Form C. 2118

16 Cheshire Regt

VOL 9

WAR DIARY
or
INTELLIGENCE SUMMARY
(Erase heading not required.)

Instructions regarding War Diaries and Intelligence Summaries are contained in F.S. Regs., Part II. and the Staff Manual respectively. Title Pages will be prepared in manuscript.

Place	Date	Hour	Summary of Events and Information	Remarks and references to Appendices
309/K.10.10.6			Bott. still occupies Trenches J.1. Sector E + NE ARRAS. Weather generally good. Enemy displays little activity. It is assumed the troops opposite us are returned from heavy fighting further South (Somme). We obtain and maintain the ascendancy over him in patrolling, sniping artillery + light T.M. work — he worries us a deal with heavy T.M.s. All manner of ruses + decoys are employed to trap his patrols so as to obtain identification but without success.	
14 to 18.10.16			Batt. is relieved by 11th S. Batt. Gloucester Regt. in tote - relief being completed at 10am without casualty or incident. In Reserve ARRAS — Two Coys held FORRIESTIER + BOSSU TNICHOAS redoubts + St Nicholas Village — two other Coys engaged in wiring + carrying parties. Trench Tramway commenced from CANDLE FACTORY to Front line — most four men employed on this work. Instructional classes commenced for N.C.O.s in general work + also Lewis Gun classes for all available men.	
18 to 25.10.16			Relieved Gloucester + returned to same Sector as previously occupied. Relief completed by 7.15a.m. without any happening [?] note. Dispositions of Companies as before. Hun more active with artillery + T.M.s but his ascendancy is soon wrested from him. His patrols are very seldom encountered in no Man's Land + his Sniping - Nil. Weather very cold for some few nights, later changing to warmer but wet.	
25th Hun.16			Trenches now much improved + capable of standing much knocking about + abusive weather. The enemy more active with artillery and T.M.s. Sniping too is much more lively than previously in the line — like absence of hostile patrols is distinctly noticeable. His troops are of a higher standard than were opposite this Sector previously. Artillery activity increases in reply to our organised strafes. Our front line + support trenches suffer much from his T.M.s + whizbangs. Weather becomes much more broken, rain falling heavily each day. Trenches collapse in some places as a result of inclement weather. All ranks busily engaged repairing. Casualties for period referred to above 1 Officer Wounded (on patrol) H.O.R. Killed. 17 O.R. wounded. Both sides generally more active than when Division first moved into Area.	

J. Frostington Major
Cmdg 16th Batt Cheshire Regt.

Dowball
1 sheet

J.K.
1 sheet

WAR DIARY
or
INTELLIGENCE SUMMARY
(Erase heading not required.)

Army Form C. 2118

11th = S. Batt. CHESHIRE REGT. (Vol 10)

Vol 10

Instructions regarding War Diaries and Intelligence Summaries are contained in F.S. Regs., Part II. and the Staff Manual respectively. Title Pages will be prepared in manuscript.

Place	Date	Hour	Summary of Events and Information	Remarks and references to Appendices
A.11.b.6.13.11.ab			Batt. Still occupies Sect" J.1. Trenches ARRAS. Weather much broken & cold at night. Trenches in many parts collapse owing to soft nature of ground, poor movement (done by previous occupants) & inclement weather. Much labour & time is expended in redeeming line & making trenches once more serviceable. Daily minor "shoots" are engaged in by which we suffer little retaliation. The chief feature of enemy retaliation is trench mortar which we effectively engage & silence on all occasions. The enemy indulges in little rifle & machine gunfire. Captured prisoners inform Brigade of night of usual relief when all arms are engaged in bringing fire to bear upon enemy trenches & roads leading to the line. "No Man's Land" is seldom occupied by hostile patrols — ascendancy previously gained maintained. Sniping practically nil	JAS RW RW
14.11.16.15.16			Batt. Strength Officers 17 O.R.s 729 in line — Outside trenches 10 Officers — 230 O.Rs Casualties 1 Officer killed 1 Officer wounded. 2 O.R. killed 3 wounded. Relieved by 11th S. Batt. Gloucester Regt. Battalion occupied whole-occupied billets in ARRAS (less two companies whole-occupied billets in St Nicholas & Redoubt Line. Relief completed at 10am. without casualty or incident. Billeted in ARRAS 2 Cos .. In Redoubts . 1 Coy plus 1 platoon .1. in St Nicholas Village 3 platoons.	RW
15.16.16			Batt engages on working parties in support lines. Constructing Trench Tramway &c. Two Cos in ARRAS relieved 11c two cos in Redoubts & St Nicholas Village without incident. Relief completed 7am. Batt. engaged on work in Sapphire line, Tramway & Gunmetal Trenches.	RW
17.18 19.11 23.d 23.11.30.a. 25/11/16			Relieved 11th S. Batt. Gloucester Regt. in J.1. Sect". Relief Complete without incident at 10am. Line had been much damaged during absence & enemy has been much more active with T.M's & artillery than previously. Regular shoots T.M.'s & artillery strafes were carried out under Rex arranged. These were accompanied by hot MG fire. On 11c night 25/11/16 the enemy raided trenches of batt on our left & right battalion of Bde on our right. Our left Coy. "Stood to" in readiness to counterattack if called upon. Gas was discharged heavy line from Bde. on our right - result unknown. Batt stood to in alert trench position during this operation. Support line reclaimed where possible destroyed. C.T.s to be placed in serviceable conditions.	RW RW RW

J Maw

WAR DIARY
or
INTELLIGENCE SUMMARY
(Erase heading not required.)

Army Form C. 2118

10th Batt Cheshire Regt

Instructions regarding War Diaries and Intelligence Summaries are contained in F. S. Regs., Part II. and the Staff Manual respectively. Title Pages will be prepared in manuscript.

Place	Date	Hour	Summary of Events and Information	Remarks and references to Appendices
Nov 16 23 to 30th			Weather continues very fine but afternoon cold. Every attempt made to increase comfort of men by improvements to dugouts & rebonding trails, rubbing of feet, frequent baths & issue of new clothing. Trenches suffer little from enemy strafing – T.M.s & shells falling beyond Support line & doing no damage at all. Casualties 1 officer slightly wounded (at duty). 1 O.R. Killed. 2 O.R. slightly wounded. 2 O.R. Died of wounds. 30 Wounded. 20 O.R. wounded at duty. Strength 15 Oct this 18 officers 704 O.R.s. 9 officers (6) O.R.s out of line Lt Col E.T. Saint 13th Cambridgeshire Regt took over command of the Battalion.	[signatures] K W H S M 10th Batt Cheshire Regt 10th Batt Cheshire Regt
Nov 25				

Vol XI
1st S. Bath. A.d. Reg.

WAR DIARY
or
INTELLIGENCE SUMMARY
(Erase heading not required.)

Army Form C. 2118

Place	Date	Hour	Summary of Events and Information	Remarks and references to Appendices
ARRAS 1st Dec. 3rd	Nov. 27		Lt. Col. E.T. SAINT, 1 CAMB. took over command of the Bn. Still in trenches J1 SubSector ARRAS. Casualties 1 O.R. died from wounds. 2. O.R. Wounded.	
DUIZANS	Dec. 3		Relieved in J1 SS by 1st S.A. Inf. Bn. proceeded to billets in ARRAS. W. and X. Companies marched to LOUEZ under Major Worthington, H.Q, Y. and Z Co. to DUIZANS, to work under C.E. VIIth Corps. Two days spent in cleaning up and drill.	
	" 5 to 8			
	" 8 - 31		Working parties for R.E. up to full strength available. Roadmaking, improving building dugouts, unloading trains.	
	" 14		2nd Lt. C.R. JONES joined unit on appointment to commission, from Sgt. INNIS. DRAG.	
	" 21		No 3 Platoon W. Co. under 2nd LT. H.N. HALLAM, proceeded to WANQUETIN and No 7 Platoon X Co. under 2nd LT. W.H. MITCHELL to LATTRE ST QUENTIN for work under R.E.	
	" 23		2nd Lts. R.A. McKNIGHT and H.E. MARROW joined Battalion from 3rd CHES.	
	" 27		Capt. G. PLAYFER appointed to command 105th Bn Co., 31st Div. Sept. Bn. 2nd LT. H.N. HALLAM appointed Platoon Commander in same Co., and proceeded to AVERDOINGT. 2nd LT. McKNIGHT relieved 2nd LT. HALLAM at WANQUETIN.	
	" 29		1 O.R. accidentally wounded, run over by railway truck, whilst a working party.	
	" 31		Bn. Strength. Officers 13 O.R's. 616 with unit. " 16 " 155 detached.	

E.T. Saint Lt Col.
16th (S) A. Ches. R.

1875 Wt. W593/826 1,000,000 4/15 I.B.C. & A. A.D.S.S./Forms/C. 2118.

Army Form C. 2118

Vol 12
16th (S) Batt. The Cheshire Regt.

WAR DIARY or INTELLIGENCE SUMMARY

(Erase heading not required.)

Instructions regarding War Diaries and Intelligence Summaries are contained in F. S. Regs, Part II. and the Staff Manual respectively. Title Pages will be prepared in manuscript.

Goodale & 10 K
2 sheets

Place	Date	Hour	Summary of Events and Information	Remarks and references to Appendices
DUISANS	Jan/17		Full strength Battalion available employed on working parties. O.E. VI Corps Inspection of Wt X Co engage on Bunking work under R E at LATTRE ST QUENTIN and WANQUENTIN as previous month.	
	4-1-17		Draft of 2 OR arrived	
	5-1-17		Lt J.O.W. Stonekes & 2/Lt H.S.Baxter arrived Lt Stonekes reverts to 2/Lieut. on attestation reporting 2/Lt O.W.R.D Cooper, 2/Lt W Pickford 2/Lt O.T Livinstow, 2/Lt E.D Stonelke.	
	10-1-17		2/Lt M.B Kernon reported for duty	
			Inspection rifles by Army Car. 2/Lt J W King transferred to the My Corps Heavy Branch	
	16-1-17			
	30/1/16		Authy A.G. A m/14/18832 df- 30/1/16 CR No 3682 C	
			1/Lt R.T Morris reported for duty 114 Draft arrived and sent to 35th Divisional Depot Battont A/T DOINET for training 1/Lt W Hallam transferred to My Corps Heavy Branch Authy A 3202 df- 7/1/17	
	7-1-17			

1875. Wt. W593/826 1,000,000 4/15 T.R.C. & A.   A.D.S.S./Forms/C.2118.

Army Form C. 2118

WAR DIARY
or
INTELLIGENCE SUMMARY 16 th (S) Batt. The Cheshire Regt
Continued
(Erase heading not required.)

Place	Date	Hour	Summary of Events and Information	Remarks and references to Appendices
	18-1-17		Instructional classes for all available N.C.Os. commenced at BUNEVILLE under Capt. Hodgson. 18 NCOs and 286 O.R.s arrived at BUNEVILLE and retained here for purpose of training & instruction for this purpose being detailed from the Battalion. Standard of training & efficiency of this draft who must attain the 16th minst. previous draft which arrived 16th 16th inst.	
	24-1-17		The remaining Pelham Pts. & Os. were relieved from billets at LOUEZ by the 6th Entrenching Batt.- moved to huntments at Neant-mulins DUISANS. 35 men repelled from Entrenching Batt. were sent to Junction Co. (2 July 24 /16) 211 other men repelled were sent down to the Base for employment in various capacities.	
	3-1-17		The strength of the Battalion 33 officers and 946 O.R.s	

S. Worthington Major
O.C. 16 th Batt Cheshire Regt

Army Form C. 2118

WAR DIARY
or
INTELLIGENCE SUMMARY

County 11th (S) Bn. The Cheshire Regt.

(Erase heading not required.)

Vol 13

11K.
1 sheet

Place	Date	Hour	Summary of Events and Information	Remarks and references to Appendices
DURANS	2/3/17		Battalion marched to LATTRE ST QUENTIN.	
LATTRE ST QUENTIN	3/3/17		Left LATTRE ST QUENTIN and marched to BUNEVILLE and carried on training.	
BUNEVILLE	4/3/17		" BUNEVILLE by road and to BONNIERES, LONGUEVILETTE and FLESSELLES, staying one night in each place.	
FLESSELLES	6-17/3/17		Intensive training at FLESSELLES. Lt R.C BACON, 2nd Lts J. MILLER, R.M HAMILTON, R. HORSFALL, R.J. MCCULLOUGH, joined for duty on 16/3/17.	
	18/3/17		Entrained at FLESSELLES, detrained at MARCELCAVE, and marched to DEMUIN, and billeted for the night.	
DEMUIN	19/3/17		Co. proceeded to ROSIÈRES-EN-SANTERRE, and reconnoitred new line to be taken over from the French in CHILLY Sector.	
	20/3/17		Marched to CAMPS-DES-BALLONS, 1 mile S. of CAIX, into huts for one night.	
VRELY	21/3/17		Marched to VRELY, where Battalion was in reserve to 105 Bde in CHILLY Sector.	
	22/3/17 23/3/17 to 28/3/17		Companies employed cleaning trenches, training re. reconnoitring line daily. Strength of Battalion 26 Officers 860 O.Rs.	

Sd. W. Scott
Major
Comdg. 11th (S) Bn.
The Cheshire Regt.

WAR DIARY or INTELLIGENCE SUMMARY

Army Form C. 2118

16th Cheshire Regt.   Vol /4

Place	Date	Hour	Summary of Events and Information	Remarks and references to Appendices
CAMP DES BALLOTS.	1/3/17		Relieved 15th Bn. The Cheshire Regt. in the Garrison Trenches, LEFT SUB-SECTOR, CHILLY SECTOR. Casualties: - 1 O.R. wounded by Shrapnel.	
CHILLY SECTOR.	2/3/17		2 O.R's wounded - Front line. On the night of 2nd - 3rd March, enemy raided in two places on front line, on "W" Company frontage, repulsed without enemy entering trench. On "Y" Company front. The Enemy entered the H.E., and inflicted losses as follows - 3 Officers wounded, 1 officer gassed, 6 O.R's killed, 18 O.R's wounded & gassed, and 19 O.R's missing. 1 Known enemy 1 Officer (W.Coy) gassed. From reports received it would appear that the enemy suffered severe losses during both raids. (Autry. 35719/34110/A.)	
—"—	3/3/17		2nd Lieut J.B. Kinged transferred to the Royal Flying Corps. (Auty. 35719/34110/A. of 22.2.17.)	
—"—	4/3/17		2 O.R. wounded - Front line.	
—"—	5/3/17		3 O.R. wounded - Front line.	
—"—	6/3/17		Relieved by 23rd Bn. Manchester Regt. No casualties. Marched to ROSIERES.	

WAR DIARY
or
INTELLIGENCE SUMMARY

(Erase heading not required.)

Army Form C. 2118

Place	Date	Hour	Summary of Events and Information	Remarks and references to Appendices
ROSIERES	7/3/17		Marched to CAMP DES BALLONS.	
CAMP DES BALLONS	8/3/17		Battalion resting.	
— " —	9/3/17		Battalion on Intensive training. 2/LIEUTS: H.I. MARROW and W. PICKFORD evacuated to England.	
— " —	10/3/17		Battalion on training. LIEUT. COL. B.C. DENT, THE LEICESTER REGIMENT, assumed command of the Battalion, vice LIEUT. COL. E.T. SAINT, THE CAMBRIDGESHIRE REGIMENT (T) to Divisional School.	
— " —	11/3/17		Battalion in training. 2/LIEUT. H.S. BAXTER (wounded 2/7) and 2/LIEUT. H. HORSFALL (gassed) evacuated to England.	
— " —	12/3/17		Battalion in training. 2/LIEUT. A.D.C. MASON reported for duty.	
— " —	14/3/17		Battalion marched to ROSIERES — thence per lorries proceeded to SUPPORT LINE, CHILLY SUB SECTOR, in relief of 18th Bn Highland Light Infantry. No casualties.	
CHILLY SUB SECTOR	15/3/17		Battalion on work improving trenches. Lieut. E.A. McKNIGHT (gassed 2/7)	

WAR DIARY
or
INTELLIGENCE SUMMARY.
(Erase heading not required.)

Army Form C. 2118

Place	Date	Hour	Summary of Events and Information	Remarks and references to Appendices
CHILLY SUBSECTOR	16th/3/17		Battalion on work improving lines.	
-"-	24th/3/17		Battalion moved to place shown east of HYENCOURT. (no shelter)	
HYENCOURT	24th/3/17		Battalion employed on Railway work, from CHAULNES STATION	
MESNIL LE PETIT	25/3/17		Marched to MESNIL LE PETIT, employed on Railway work 2 Kms E. of NESLE.	
-"-	27/3/17		On Railway work E. of NESLE. 2/LIEUTS. R.C. SEAL, C.W. McSYMON and G.L. TROUGHTON reported for duty.	
-"-	31/3/17		On Railway work E. of NESLE. Strength. 35 Officers 634 O.R's.	

B. Dent. Major.
Comdg. 16 Bn. H. Chesh. Regt.

16th Cheshire Regt

McGordy
13.K.
6 sheet.

Vol 15

WAR DIARY
or
INTELLIGENCE SUMMARY
(Erase heading not required.)

Army Form C. 2118

Instructions regarding War Diaries and Intelligence Summaries are contained in F. S. Regs., Part II. and the Staff Manual respectively. Title Pages will be prepared in manuscript.

Place	Date	Hour	Summary of Events and Information	Remarks and references to Appendices
MESNIL LE PETIT.	1/4/17		Working on railway at crater 2 kilometres E of NESLE.	
	2/4/17		Battalion marched from MESNIL-LE-PETIT, to OFFOY. 2/Lt D. Clarke reported for duty. 5 O.R's arrived from Base.	
OFFOY	3/4/17		Practice attack scheme.	
	4/4/17		Work on railway from HOMBLEUX Stn to Jello post 4.5½ mile S.W. of CANIZY.	
	5/4/17			
	6/4/17			
	7/4/17		Training. Practice attack scheme.	
	8/4/17		Work on railway as for 4th, 5th & 6th.	
	9/4/17		Training.	
	10/4/17		Work on Roads near CROIX MOLIGNAUX. 2/Lt T.C. Wood reported for duty. 112 O.R's arrived from Base.	
	11/4/17		Training.	

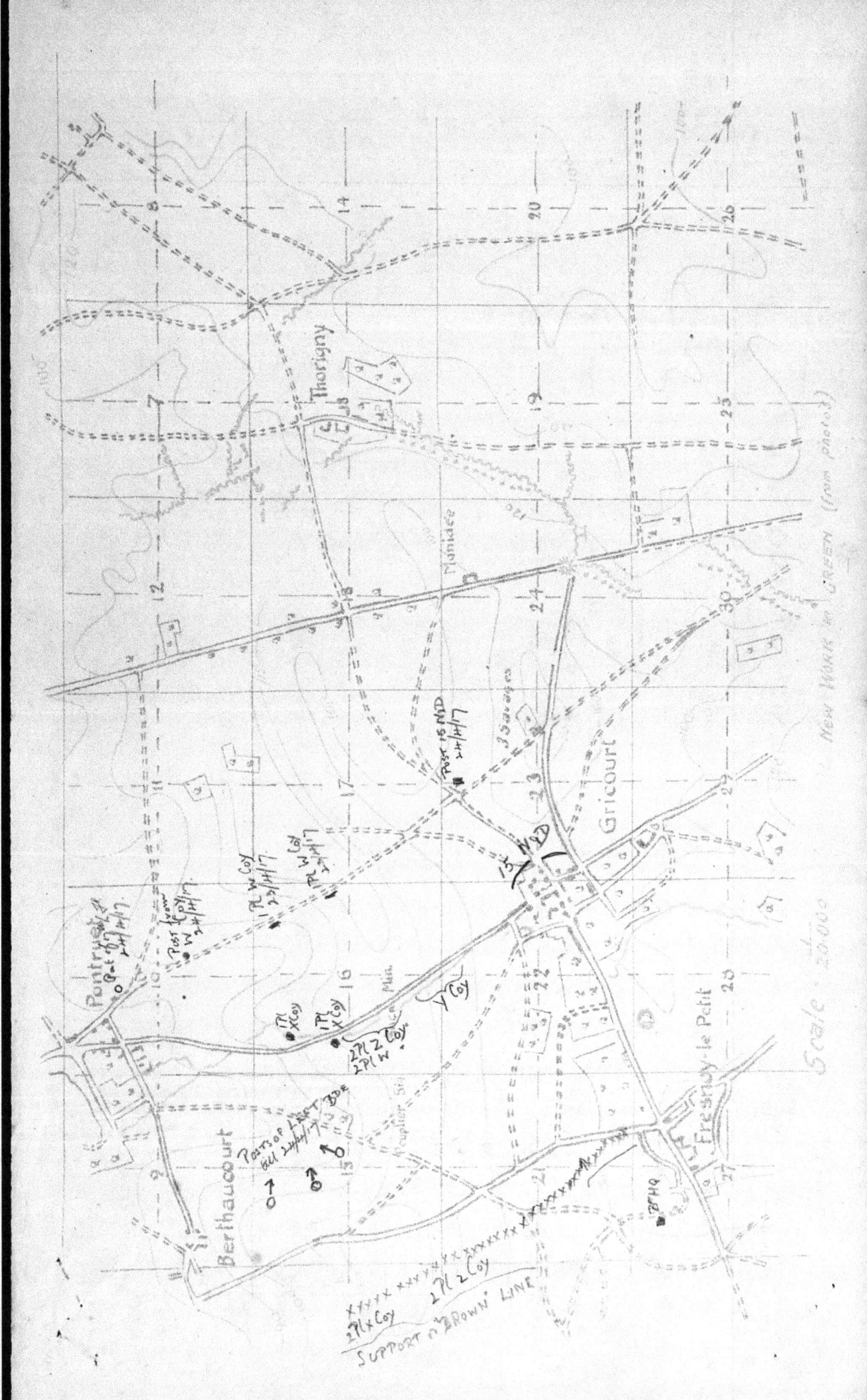

Army Form C. 2118

WAR DIARY
or
INTELLIGENCE SUMMARY

(Erase heading not required.)

Place	Date	Hour	Summary of Events and Information	Remarks and references to Appendices
OFFOY	12/4/17		Battalion moved to MONCHY-LAGACHE & MERAU COURT. X, Y & Z Companies at MONCHY. HQ & W Company at MERAU COURT.	
MONCHY LAGACHE & MERAU COURT	13/4/17		Training.	
	14/4/17.		Work on roads – Two companies on VERMAND – POEUILLY & two companies VILLEVÊQUE – MARTEVILLE road, after work moved to bivouacs at VILLEVÊQUE.	
VILLEVÊQUE	15/4/17.		Work on roads as for 14th.	
	16/4/17.		Moved to MAISSEMY & to become left support battalion to 15th Battalion (right brigade). HQ & 1 company in MAISSEMY, three companies bivouaced in valley. R29.A.3.6. (Ref sheet 62c S.E.) Brigade holding front from S.E. end of GRICOURT to about M.16.a.28 (Ref sheet 62B S.W.20000). B being right Brigade of the Division, 15th Cheshires being in left subsector of front line & 14th Cheshires in right subsector. 106th Inf. Bde. being left Brigade.	
MAISSEMY	17/4/17		Three companies worked nightly at improving the support (N BROWN) line from Northern corner of PRESNOY-LE-PETIT exclusive to M20.6.38 (Ref sheet 62B S.W.20000). Casualties: 17th – 1 O.R. killed,	
	18/4/17		1 O.R. wounded, 18th – 1 O.R. killed, 1 O.R. wounded,	
	19/4/17		19th – NIL –	

WAR DIARY
or
INTELLIGENCE SUMMARY

Army Form C. 2118

Place	Date	Hour	Summary of Events and Information	Remarks and references to Appendices
MASSENY	20/4/17		Relieved 15th Bn Cheshire Regt. in front line - 18th Bn. being on our left.	
FRONT LINE	21/4/17		Lt & Adjt C.E.E. Heywood, 2/Lt C.R. Jones & No 9725 Cpl. Leek carried out a skillful reconnaissance of sunken road N.16.6.9.1 to N.16.6.5.4, which was held by Germans C/a an advanced post. 15th Bn Notts & Derby Regt. relieved 1st Bn Glosters Regt. on our right.	
	22/4/17	4 P.M	Two platoons Z Company raided sunken road mentioned about. Enemy took place at close quarters & several Germans were seen to fall including two officers. One prisoner wounded 452nd I.R. Capt C. Slwela 2/Lt R.T. Morris wounded with 1 prisoner (wounded). O.R. 3 Missing, believed prisoner. O.R. 1 killed. Our casualties wounded.	
	23/4/17	1.30 A.M	W Company attacked sunken road in N.16. & but found it unoccupied. Posts of 1 platoon each were established at N.16.6.9.1 & N.16.6.5.4 - 15th Notts Derby established a post at N.23.6.8.1 17th Lan Fus (10th & 13th) relieved 17 R.Scots (106th Bde) on our left - Lt & Adjt C.E.E. Heywood was out by shrapnel at Battalion HQ - 17th Lan Fus to establish posts during the night at N.E. end of	
PONTRUET	24/4/17		W Company established a post about N.10.d.2.8 in touch with them - W Company heavily shelled during the day also Battn HQ at N.27.a.5.7.	

Army Form C. 2118

WAR DIARY
or
INTELLIGENCE SUMMARY
(Erase heading not required.)

Place	Date	Hour	Summary of Events and Information	Remarks and references to Appendices
FRONTLINE	25/4/17		Relieved by 15th Bn Ches Regt & went into support at MAISSEMY as on 16th.	
MAISSEMY	26/4/17		Three companies working by night giving support line FRESNOY - M21a 5.2 (Off map sheet 62S W Somme)	
	27/4/17		Three companies working by night improving & wiring support line FRESNOY - M21a 7.4.	
	28/4/17		The battalion was ordered to attack copse in M11.d (Ref sheet 62SW Somme) which had been reported strongly held on previous night. W, X, Y companies assembled in sunken road M16c, & moved thence to point of departure in front of sunken road in M16.6. X & Y companies lined out as assaulting companies single Capt. G.P. Hay in command company in front of two platoons. W Coy in Each coy on a front of two platoons. X & Y coys in reserve in sunken road in M16b. Assembly was completed at 1.4am & came under rifle & M.G. fire at 1.19am.	
	29/4/17		Our barrage commenced at 1.19am. Attempt our guns put down a creeping barrage between M17.c.5.5 9 M17.9 at 1.19am. This barrage lifted 100 yds every 3 minutes. A slow clay barrage was put on enemy main trench between M17.c.5.1 & M17.6.5.1 from 1.19am to 2.15am.	

WAR DIARY or INTELLIGENCE SUMMARY

Army Form C. 2118

Place	Date	Hour	Summary of Events and Information	Remarks and references to Appendices
MASSEMY	29/4/17		The assaulting Companies carried the wood & killed some Germans in it, about six prisoners showed up about 50 yds to NE of wood. A patrol from each company was then sent out towards German wire. The enemy put up a barrage behind in assaulting companies for NE and further not in M16b. But stopped when our guns stopped. The assaulting companies watched consolidated & relieved by patrols. A search party of departure at 3.30am. Enemy Gun barrages.	
			Wounded Officers 1, OR 7, + 2 subsequently reported killed. OR 26 + 2 Died of wounds. Wounded OR's 78. Missing OR 2	
		1.40pm	2/Lt R.D.S. Everard reported for duty.	
			2/Lt A.C. Wood & 2/Lt R.D.S. Everard reported for duty.	
	30/4/17		Strength of Battalion:— Officers 40, OR's 781 Battalion relieved by 17th Batt Royal Scots & marched to Camp at TREPCON during the afternoon.	

B.C. Dent. Lt Col.
Commdg 16th Bn Cheshire Regt

WAR DIARY or **INTELLIGENCE SUMMARY**

Army Form C. 2118

16th Cheshire

Place	Date	Hour	Summary of Events and Information	Remarks and references to Appendices
TREFCON S.F. Alphabet 62c	1/5/17		Battalion living in tents at TREFCON while Brigade was in Divisional Reserve. Two Companies training - Two Companies work on Roads.	
	2/5/17		Training.	
	3/5/17		Training - Battalion attack Scheme.	
	4/5/17		Training - Battalion attack Scheme.	
	5/5/17		Training.	
	6/5/17		Two Companies training Two Companies on roads, as for 1/5/17	
	7/5/17		Training.	
	8/5/17		Training.	
FRESNOY Sector of line Alphabet 2M	9/5/17 10/5/17 11/5/17		The Battalion relieved the 17th (S) Bn Royal Scots (106th Inf Bde) in the left subsector of FRESNOY sector. (Ref map sheet 62B S.W.) Battalion in the front line. During this period a relief kitchen & Companies were carried out. There were now 2 outpost Companies holding between them 3 piquets, one Company in close support in CHALK LINE & 1 Company in Reserve in BROWN LINE -	
MASSENY	12/5/17		Relieved Aug 15th (S) Bn Ches Regt & proceeded to MASSENY as Battalion in reserve. Bn HdQrs & 1 Company in the village, 2 Companies in valley behind village & 1 Company in BROWN LINE NORTH of BERTAUCOURT. Casualties O.R 6 Wounded O.R 4 - 12th inclusive	14 T F Shields

WAR DIARY
or
INTELLIGENCE SUMMARY
(Erase heading not required.)

Army Form C. 2118

Place	Date	Hour	Summary of Events and Information	Remarks and references to Appendices
MAISSEMY	15/5/17 15/5/17 15/5/17		Two Companies doing each night in front of sunken road in M.I.6. (Ref Maps sheet 62.S.W.)	
FRESNOY Section of front line	16/5/17		Relieved 158th Bn The Cheshire Regt in left subsector FRES NOY sector - Major R Watkinson 2nd in Command of the Battalion lines July 1915 was killed while going the round of the posts at PONTRUET.	
	18/5/17		Preparation for relief by the French - Stuart Bell Commanded 9 officers per company & 1 NCO per platoon came up in advance to take on etc.	
	19/5/17		Battn relieved by 2nd Battn 91st French Infantry Regiment. During relief there was an incident at Post No 34 - as follows. Owing to the jitters of the night the garrison of the post did not go out to occupy it until about 10 p.m. When garrison got within a short distance of post they it was bombed by surprise by Germans who had already occupied the post. Our party (which counted 1 NCO & 6 men suffered 6 Casualties (wounded) and was forced to	

WAR DIARY
or
INTELLIGENCE SUMMARY
(Erase heading not required.)

Army Form C. 2118

Place	Date	Hour	Summary of Events and Information	Remarks and references to Appendices
FRESNOY Active patrolling			go back to Stopyuet. Patrols at about 12.30am the Post was occupied by its garrison without opposition, the German party which was observed to be resting near Solosmo men having retired. The relief by French was completed without further incident at 2 am.	
	20/5/17		The Battalion proceeded to SOYÉ COURT via VILLECHOLLES on relief.	
SOYÉCOURT			SOYÉCOURT, Bn HQ D3 companies in valley S.W. of 1 Company in SOYÉCOURT. Capt. W. Hodson M.C. (15th Bn Chos Regt) reported for duty as 2nd in command vice Major R. Worthington - Killed in action.	
	21/5/17		Battalion was given almost a complete rest - Impromptu Concerts were arranged for both evenings. 9 on afternoon of 22nd we had Battalion Sports. There was also bathing in CAULAINCOURT LAKE.	
	22/5/17			
PERONNE	23/5/17		Battalion moved to billets in PERONNE during the afternoon - Lt Col B.C. Dent took temporary command of 105th Infantry Brigade & Major W. Hodson M.C. became temporarily in command of the Battalion.	
	24/5/17		Battalion at PERONNE.	
	25/5/17		Battalion moved during the evening to camp near TEMPLEUX-LA-FOSSÉ. D.29.d.9.2. of Map sheet 62 c. 9 became part of Brigade in Divisional Reserve.	

WAR DIARY
or
INTELLIGENCE SUMMARY

(Erase heading not required.)

Army Form C. 2118

Place	Date	Hour	Summary of Events and Information	Remarks and references to Appendices
TEMPLEUX LA FOSSE	26/5/17		Two Companies Training - Two Companies working -	
	27/5/17		Inoculation & training.	
	28/5/17		Training & Bathing - 2/Lt R Makin, 2/Lt A.W. Owen, 2/Lt W.G. Agnew, 2/Lt G.S. Waltho reported for duty from hos. I.B.D.	
	29/5/17		Training	
	30/5/17		Training	
	31/5/17		Brigade attack scheme with Contact aeroplane. 2/Lt W. Mitchell proceeded to England to Engineer Crude at NEWARK.	
			Strength of Battalion 31/5/17. Officers 38 O.R. 712	

M.N. Norris Major
Comdg 16th Ches Regt

16th Bn The Cheshire Regt.

105th Infantry Brigade

Herewith "War Diary" of
16th Bn. The Cheshire Regt
for Month of June 1917

Gordon Harper
Capt
a/adjt.
16 Bn The Cheshire Rgt

2/7/17

WAR DIARY or INTELLIGENCE SUMMARY

Army Form C. 2118.

16 Bn L Cheshire Regt.

Jun 17

15K
5 sheets

Place	Date	Hour	Summary of Events and Information	Remarks and references to Appendices
TEMPLEUX la FOSSE.	1/6/17	—	Company training carried out.	
	2/6/17	—	Inspection of Trench Stores preparatory to relief of 1/8 N.F. (Reserve Bn - Right sub sector Divisional Front) at VAUCELETTE Fm - 2/Lt R.M. HAMILTON took over duties of acting Adjutant during 2/Lt R.P. HARRISON's absence on leave - Relief complete about 11.40 p.m.	
	3/6/17	—	100 O.R. + 3 Officers detailed for security duty to 178th Tunnelling Coy R.E. 2/Lt HAMILTON accompany Recon Survey and Retirer attd 11.50 a.m. - Night work - Smith - Y Coy - Green Lane - W + X Coy - Reserve Line - CAPTAIN PLAYFER assumed acting Adjt.	
	4/6/17	—	W. + Y. Coys nothing by day - working by night Co op 3/6/17	
	5/6/17	—	Lt Col. L.G. Best returned from Brigade & resumed command of the Bn.	
	6/6/17	—	W + X + Y Coys - Nothing by day - working by night continuing work coop 6/6/17 Major T.C. BOWE evacuated to U.K. (S) 3/6/17. 2/Lt J.P. FLYNN to R.F.C. (5/6/17)	
	7/6/17 8/6/17 9/6/17	—	Working parties continued - VILLERS GUISLAIN occasionally shelled	
	10/6/17	—	Preparation for relief of 15th Bn Che Regt.	
	11/6/17	—	2 p.m. Relief complete without incident - 3 Coys in front line W Right dummy cavalry X Centre Y Left joining 15th Bn Ntle & Seaby Z Support. VILLERS GUISLAIN shelled 5 p.m. - 5.30 p.m.	

WAR DIARY
or
INTELLIGENCE SUMMARY.
(Erase heading not required.)

Army Form C. 2118.

Place	Date	Hour	Summary of Events and Information	Remarks and references to Appendices
VILLERS GUISLAIN	11/6/19	—	Trenches in poor condition - Front line Coys working hard on same - Support Companys moving in front of Right Coy - work could only be carried out with safety in trenches under cover of darkness	
	12/6/19	—	Blower Station. Enemy LTM active on our right Coy (W) - No damage done - activity checked upon our Artillery opening fire - Work on trenches continued - Pack mules used to take Coy rations up to Front Line - Parties went out from each Coy in the front line - ground reconnoitred - No unusual incidents took place.	
	13/6/19	—	Enemy quiet - Work continued - Patrol from right Coy under 2/Lt Minorio endeavoured to reconnoitre Route, but were heavily fired at by Enemy M.G.	
	14/6/19	—	MAJOR W. HODSON M.C. (2nd in Command) Evac 555 CCS - Our Artillery carried out bombardment of RES TRANCHEES during night. Enemy nothing ud/15 - Work on trench work continued	
	15/6/19	—	Quiet day - Work on trench work continued - work cleaning great improvement.	
	16/6/19	—	Commanding officer & Coy Commdrs of relieving unit - 17th L.F. came to reconnaitre line - Quiet day - Work on Trench work continued	
	17/6/19	—	Still Quiet - works continued - 11 ft. Arthurs shed on HONNE COURT WOOD for 15 mins - no damage. A patrol from Y Coy of 25 O.R. under 2/Lt. A.C. WOOD attempted to enter HONNECOURT WOOD from N.W. edge at 11.20 p.m.	

Army Form C. 2118.

WAR DIARY
or
INTELLIGENCE SUMMARY.
(Erase heading not required.)

Instructions regarding War Diaries and Intelligence Summaries are contained in F.S. Regs., Part II. and the Staff Manual respectively. Title pages will be prepared in manuscript.

Place	Date	Hour	Summary of Events and Information	Remarks and references to Appendices
VILLERS GUISLAIN	17/6/17	—	At the Bomb bore a similar party from X Coy under 2/Lt HASLER attempted to enter enemy front line trenches. Strong opposition. Heavy gun fire encountered. No operations were made. No casualties. Strong opposition. Heavy gun fire encountered. No operations were made. No damage was done to the enemy by our artillery fire. Left L.O. line. Bomb & Rifle Grenades - casualties - slight 2 O.R. k. & slight wdd. & slight wounds.	
	18/6/17	—	Quiet day. Relieved parts of relieving front arrived in afternoon. Relief completed about midnight without incident - Trenches handed over in good condition. Guards & church walked - civilian buried works.	
TEMPLEUX LA FOSSE	19/6/17	—	Bn. reached Camp 4.50 a.m. Remainder of day Resting - Cleaning etc. - Congratulatory message received from French & taking over FRESNOY Sect. Communicated to men separately and also Divisional Guard. Also from the G.O.C. N.Y. reference to be shown. Made Division Order.	
	20/6/17	—	Ordinary training - Lectures etc. - Concentrate on Musketry - Bayonet fighting & 2/Lt HARRISON - absent - Could adjusted.	
	21/6/17	—	Training continues - Musketry - Bayonet fighting - Physical & Platoon attacks etc.	
	22/6/17	—	do	
	23/6/17	—	Ath. inspection P.O.W.S. Proof of O.R. as usual - Lectures etc. air. 3 officers 42 O.R.	

Army Form C. 2118.

WAR DIARY
or
INTELLIGENCE SUMMARY.
(Erase heading not required.)

Instructions regarding War Diaries and Intelligence Summaries are contained in F.S. Regs., Part II. and the Staff Manual respectively. Title pages will be prepared in manuscript.

Place	Date	Hour	Summary of Events and Information	Remarks and references to Appendices
TEMPLEUX la FOSSE	22/4/17		Officers with reinforcement - 2/Lt F PANTER 2/Lt H.K. HEMINGWAY 2/Lt G.A. SHANNON	
	24/6/17		Lecture by ADMS on Sanitation also by Brig Gen. on Trench Discipline. Major W. HODSON M.C.	
			re'td from hospital & resumed duties of Second in Command.	
	24/6/17		Training carried out to usual syll. CHURCH PARADE 8 A.M.	
	25/6/17		Training carried on - Brig Gen inspected chapl of 1/5 O.R. - MAJOR HODSON M.C. arranged action	
			of relief of 1/8 R.W.F.	
	26/6/17		Training as usual until 1 p.m. Afternoon inspection of trench stores & arrangts for journey.	
			We proceeded in coy's by ADMS & proceeded to BASE Bn Hd.Qrs W/ O.C. Relief complete	
			with'ut incident 11.30 P.M. Lt Col DG Oaks arrived at England on leave - MAJOR	
			W. HODSON assumed command.	
REVELON	27/6/17		Y Coy Brown Lane Z Coy MORRIS BANK W + X Coys - BROWN LINE - Return to coy hdqts	
			Wright - Detailed duties on Dug Outs - assemble of B.G. on two front line trench	
			(arranged Lt 106 Bde)	
	28/6/17		Do	
	29/6/17		Do	
	30/6/17		To SOYECOURT Sta bus going to Dieppe going out of date 1/7/17	

M.M. [signature]
A/Lt. Col.
Comdg 2/5[?]

Army Form C. 2118.

16th Bn. CHESHIRE REGT.

WO/8

WAR DIARY
or
INTELLIGENCE SUMMARY

(Erase heading not required.)

16 K.
Achuts

Place	Date	Hour	Summary of Events and Information	Remarks and references to Appendices
REVELON	1/7/17		At 7.48 A.M. the Enemy attempted to raid 11th Bn. the Gloster Regt. the Battalion stood to, ready to counter attack until 2.32 P.M.	
VILLERS FAUCON	2/7/17		March and the Battalion bivouaced during the day to settle at VILLERS FAUCON. Ordinary training carried out succeeding on Musketry and School fighting &c.	
	3/7/17		Ordinary training on the Balloon wood through sack and full gear kills &c	
	4/7/17		Select of Infantry scouts away for Corps CSSUS &c.	
	5/7/17		Select of Infantry scouts away for Div CSSUS &c.	
	6/7/17		Batty 1 Corporal to Q.2 Bombing school about midnight. Heavy Shelling near Dugout	
MIDDLE POST	7/7/17		Quarry for a few minutes resulting in one slight casualty. One X by the Cavalry	
EPEHY	8/7/17		Brigade commenced both L & [?] up the L OSTS. Sort of [?].	
See/in	9/7/17		2nd Lt. M.R. BARBER wounded by bullet whilst on the Q.B.D. together with Cpl. CAMERON Pte.	
			on patrol the North between OSTS entered	
	10/7/17		Work continued. Fire in hut of "B" Coys 3rd and CSSUS to entrained	
	11/7/17		Work entrained also the last Battalion L.O. connected. One O.R. wounded in action	
	12/7/17		Work continued — ??? Officer ill on trench with TWO Sept limbs Enemy attempted Raid on the 15th Bn. SHERWOODS at BIRD CAGE POST without success Barrage was preventing severe — Y company under Capt BURNETT were protecting	

WAR DIARY or INTELLIGENCE SUMMARY

Army Form C. 2118.

1st Bn. E. Cheshire Regt.

Place	Date	Hour	Summary of Events and Information	Remarks and references to Appendices
KILDARE POST	13/7/17		Covering parties for the 5th Bn Cheshire Regt. stayed out until situation became restored and showed much coolness. Casualties 2 killed & 4 wounded. The Northumberland W.D. and the Grenades suffered somewhat heavy casualties. Communication was kept through out between RSM posts Bn HQ and Brigade. Casualties 1 2 3 4 and Bn H.Q. and also between Br H.Q. and Brigade.	
	14/7/17		At light long ranging patrols were sent out. They returned without incident. During the afternoon 2nd Lieut D.W. Mills and 3 O.R. got a good daylight patrol. Sent on his eve entered Boche trenches but time not sufficient to look out decent details. Lieut. General Major General Franks CB visited Bn. H.Q. Commanding Officer sent to transport lines but high eccent. O.C. 23rd Manchester and his orderly reconnoitred line	
	15/7/17		Relief completed by 23rd Manchester and Battalion marched without incident - Quiet night	
AIZECOURT LES BAS	16/7/17		Battalion marched and at Aizecourt le Bas at 4-15 a.m. Hot cloudy weather	
	17/7/17		Musketry - Lewis Gun and Bayonet Instruction. Bn. shooting at night	
	18/7/17		Training continued Concert by Battalion concert troops at night	
	19/7/17		do Football Match at night 1st Battalion East Cheshires vs Brigade HQ	

2 - 1

WAR DIARY
or
INTELLIGENCE SUMMARY.

Army Form C. 2118.

16th Bn. The Cheshire Regt

Place	Date	Hour	Summary of Events and Information	Remarks and references to Appendices
	19/7/17		Bn Orders republished extract from London Gazette — "16th Bn Cheshire Regt." being read to at Coys. Stations. R.S. BRON Jany 1st 1917. — G.S. MEN Feby 12th 1917. —	
AIZECOURT le BAS	20/7/17		Training — Battalion Attack — Bullet Bayonet — Shooting condition at light	
	21/7/17		Training continued Company Attacks — Musketry — Bullet Bayonet — too hot to leave E. Burrows. Coy.	
	22/7/17		Burrows son 5 goals 2 tr — Six CHURKAS Brigade Cinema course. Inspection by Brigadier General L to Eastern Brigade. Shooting condition — No 13 Saloon under Lieut D.W. Mills obtained 2nd best the second in command and Coolant Watson reconnoitred new sections to Battalion cinema Kent gave a Concert — Kept quiet — At night	
	23/7/17		Rely of 1/8th Bn Coat Yorks in C. Sect — Kept Quiet — 10.25 am Lieut Col B.C. DENT transferred to B.C.C.S sick P.U.O. Battery of 1 R.G.A in small wood West of Bn HQ nearly shelled by enemy West Artillery — Excellent shooting 2 G.P enclosed several Casualties.	
QUARRY BN HQ F.27.c.d a Secta.	24/7/17		At light 2nd Lieut WALTRO C.F. had a mistake accident. Lost shoulder — X.Y.Z. Company in bathing parties in front line — W. Company being at F. Lewing Musketry Camp — Bn REST since 18/7/17	
EMPIRE Sect.	25/7/17		Quiet during day — bathing parties for light as on night of 24/7/17	

WAR DIARY
or
INTELLIGENCE SUMMARY.
(Erase heading not required.)

Army Form C. 2118.

16 Bn S. Cheshire R.

Place	Date	Hour	Summary of Events and Information	Remarks and references to Appendices
QUARRY	26/7/17	26/7/17	Work of deepening and widening front line trenches continued. — Partly by day and partly by night.	
	3/7/17		"D" Company returned from South Camp Meteren School after a course of 10 days.	
	3/7/17		Relief by 2 L.I. postponed. Battalion informed that they will be relieved night 13th-August by 11th Suffolks - 34th Division	

M Wakam Major
Commanding. 16 Bn S. Cheshire Regt.

WAR DIARY or INTELLIGENCE SUMMARY

Army Form C. 2118.

16th Bn Cheshire R.   Vol 17

Place	Date	Hour	Summary of Events and Information	Remarks and references to Appendices
QUARRY.	1/8/17		Advance parties of the 11th Suffolks took over PIMPLE, TOINE, ORCHARD & BASSE BOULOGNE (SOUTH) POSTS. & the Battalion was relieved during the evening. The Battalion marched to Camp at TEMPLEUX LA FOSSE.	
TEMPLEUX LA FOSSE.	2/8/17		Resting & Cleaning up. 2nd Lt W.G. HASLER left to join RFC	
	3/8/17		Training was carried out during the morning, the afternoon being devoted to inter & coy games. The Battalion Concert party rechristened the "ACORNS" gave a special entertainment during the evening.	
	4/8/17		Church parade. Pool shooting in the evening.	
	5/8/17		Training continued. Working parties were supplied by X Y/Companies to prepare ground for practice attack on KNOLL.	
	6/8/17		Training continued. Lt Col B.C. DENT returned to Battn from Corps Convalescent depôt.	
	7/8/17		X & Z Coys took part in practice attack against the proposed perimeter. The remainder of the Battn watched for instruction.	
	8/8/17		Heats for Brigade Sports were played. Z Coy running their way to the Semi Final of football match.	

WAR DIARY

16th Bn Cheshire Regt

Army Form C. 2118.

INTELLIGENCE SUMMARY

Place	Date	Hour	Summary of Events and Information	Remarks and references to Appendices
Templeux la Fosse	9/8/17		X & Z Coy took part in an early morning attack on the proposed positions. The remainder of the Batt. carried on training. In the afternoon teams were selected for Brigade Sports. Try-outs were pulled & resulted in a win for 15th B. SHERWOODS. Post shooting took place from 5.6 P.M. Advance parties to take over the outpost-line were sent off at 10 a.m.	
	10/8/17		Brigade sports were held at 2 P.M. The Batt: won the repeat fire competition with excellent score — rounds fired 261, score 629, actual 3½, total 625½, the Prize for this competition was a silver bugle & money given by the Brigadier. The 15th Sherwoods won second with a score of 593½. In the evening the Batt: was conveyed to L'EPINE by motor lorry, thence they marched to take over the battle front. W Cy & FLEECEALL & EGO pnts, X Coy to SART LANE & cellars in LEMPIRE, Y Coy to GRAFTONPost, Z Coy in reserve to each LEMPIRE CENTRAL & EAST, YAK, & ZEBRA pnts. Bn H.Qrs in Lempire.	
LEMPIRE	11/8/17		Quiet day. Work carried out wiring & improving trenches.	
	13/8/17		Quiet day. Bomb accident in X Coy killed 3 O.R. Wounded (not duty) Z Cy relieved W Cy in Fleeceall & Ego pnts.	
	14/8/17			

WAR DIARY 16th Bn. Cheshire Regt.
INTELLIGENCE SUMMARY

Army Form C. 2118.

3

Place	Date	Hour	Summary of Events and Information	Remarks and references to Appendices
LEMPIRE	15/8/17		2/Lt LAWRENSON & 2 O.R. wounded while out with a party carrying 2 Coys of Pioneer Bn. at work on BANK TRENCH.	
	16/8/17		A new post established at junction of BANK TRENCH & FAG LANE to relieve ISLAND TRAVERSE. Continued work on trenches.	
	17/8/17		W.Coy relieved two platoons Z Coy & took over BANK TRENCH, ISLAND TRAVERSE, F1, F2, F3, & EGO POSTS.	
	18/8/17		Capt. & Acting G. PLAYFER granted Special Leave. X & Z Coys reconnoitred routes to the KNOLL & prepared same. At dusk snipers & Lewis guns covered W.Cy supplied patrols & carrying parties.	
	19/8/17		At 4 am the 13th Cheshires & 15th Sherwoods attacked the KNOLL being brought up by carrying parties supplied by W.Cy. When the objective was taken X & Z Cys carried ammunition &c. to the KNOLL with remarkable success. Presently enemy fire was directed to the KNOLL during S Prior to moving up Z Cy were caught by enemy barrage & Capt. BACON 7/C Cy & C.S.M. HUGHES were both wounded. Our total casualties were 3 Officers Capt. BACON, 2/Lt JOHNSTON, 2/Lt MILLER (at Arty) & 11 other ranks wounded. 2/Lt R.D. HOWELLS & 1 O.R. W.Cy were wounded on special Recce under N° 6 for going patrol work.	
	20/8/17		Artillery active. k SOS from KNOLL on three occasions. No enemy counter attacks succeeded. Y Cy relieved W.Cy who had been heavily shelled this Casualties were Lt Killed, 1 Died of Wounds, 3 wounded in 12 - 24 hours Pts Killed & Wounded & c in 12 - 24 hours.	

Army Form C. 2118.

16" B. Cheshire R.

4

WAR DIARY
or
INTELLIGENCE SUMMARY.

(Erase heading not required.)

Place	Date	Hour	Summary of Events and Information	Remarks and references to Appendices
LEMPIRE	21/8/17		Counter attack against KNOLL repld Flammenwerfer reported by Sherwoods.	
	22/8/17		Day Operational quiet. The Bn. was relieved by 1st GLOUSTERS & marched to camp at St EMILIE.	
St EMILIE	23/8/17		The Bn rested. At a performance by the "Acorns" the Commanding Officer read out congratulatory messages from Staff of 2nd Army, 3rd Corps, 35 Div, & 105th Brigade. He also presented the "Rapid Fire" Team with Silver Bugle & the money prizes won at Brigade Sports.	
	24/8/17		The Bn. turned the South side of COCHRAN AV from the KNOLL towards FAG LANE.	
	25/8/17		The Bn. relieved the 13th SHERWOODS who had been heavily shelled on the KNOLL. Y & Z Coys on the KNOLL, X Coy in SART LANE, W Coy in Sunken Road N.W. of LEMPIRE. Bn. H.Q. in Heccall Post.	
	26/8/17		Day quiet. Y & Z Coys suffering 5 casualties. W Coy relieved Y Coy & X Coy relieved Z Coy with no incident. A party of X Coy under Sgt WILKINSON attempted to reach the Block north by the enemy & the trench of DEANPRE. Six died Germans were seen. No Cheris. Casualties.	
	27/8/17		Day quiet. Bn. was relieved by 12th Bn. W. Yorks & proceeded to Camps at TEMPLEUX LA FOSSE	
TEMPLEUX LA FOSSE	28/8/17		The Bn. rested during the day.	
	29/8/17		Platoon inspections were held. Foot about during took place in the evening.	

WAR DIARY 16th B. Cheshire R.
or
INTELLIGENCE SUMMARY

Army Form C. 2118.
5

Place	Date	Hour	Summary of Events and Information	Remarks and references to Appendices
TEMPEUX LA FOSSE	30/8/17		The Commanding Officer inspected the Battn. by Companies in the evening. Inter Company Shooting Competition was won by Z Coy. Post shooting, revolver shooting for Officers also took place.	
	31/8/17		Brigadier's congratulatory address by Corps Commander. During the night the Battn. were ordered to stand by ready to move at one hours notice.	

B. C. Newstead
Comdg 16th (S) 16th
Cheshire Regt

WAR DIARY
OR
INTELLIGENCE SUMMARY.

(Erase heading not required.)

10TH (SERVICE) BATTN CHESHIRE REGT.

September

Army Form C. 2118.

Place	Date	Hour	Summary of Events and Information	Remarks and references to Appendices
AZECOURT	1/9/17		Battalion proceeded into camp at St Emilie as Brigade Reserve.	
ST EMILIE	2/9/17 to 5/9/17		100 Companies supplied working parties by day between GUILLEMONT FARM and ISLAND TRAVERSE	
	6/9/17		Battalion relieved 14th the Gloster Regt in Bde - Spt - Bt GUILLEMONT &c.	
	7/9/17		Frontage quiet with exception of a few heavy trench mortars.	
	8/9/17		"C" Company working party under Lieut Barber attempted a small raid on Enemy Sap but owing to post being uncut found it necessary to withdraw without loss. Later in the morning the farm was heavily bombarded with heavy trench mortars. Mortar, one man being wounded. Lieut Barber also wounded in attempting to recover one of the bodies.	
			Battalion informed of following awards:- Lieut Barber - Military Cross - Sergt Brown - Sergt Hay - Privt Clarke, Privt Turner, Privt Walters - all Bart Post - Military Medals.	
	10/9/17		5 Officers & O.R. proceeded to England on leave. Line quiet - Officers & 17th Lancashire Fusiliers reconnoitred line preparatory to relief.	
	11/9/17		2 N.W. Bart Post heavily shelled owing to operations of 24th Division on right.	
	12/9/17		2 P.M. Bart Post again heavily shelled - aerial attack by 23rd Division.	
			Relief carried out without incident on relief by 17th Lancashire Fusiliers.	

WAR DIARY
or
INTELLIGENCE SUMMARY.   16TH (SERVICE) BATTN CHESHIRE REGT.

September

Army Form C. 2118.

Place	Date	Hour	Summary of Events and Information	Remarks and references to Appendices
AIZECOURT	13/10/17		Battalion reached Camp at AIZECOURT by 3.10 A.M. Rest – Bathing &c – Inspections by Company Commanders. Lecture by Brigadier General about "Rusting".	
	14/10/17		Musketry – Bullet Survey. Meeting by Officers and Sergeants Continued. Lt Col Kent acting Brigadier whilst Brigadier General on Leave.	
	15/10/17		Training continued – Recreation – Football and Concert by "Horros". Capt by Horros.	
	16/10/17		Training continued – Captain Ewden Porter Commanding the Battalion.	
	17/10/17		Reconnoitred ASSUS POSTS preparatory to relief.	
	18/10/17	19/10/17 20/10/17	Battalion relieved 17th Royal Scots about midnight – X Company ASSUS POSTS 3,4. Z Company ASSUS POSTS 1, 2. Line quiet. W Company and Y Company W. Coy. V. Coy. in support.	
ADELPHI			Working out Tunnelling Company on PIGEON QUARRY.	
	21/10/17		W. Company Loving in part of W & J. FRENCH – Y Company working MOORE LANE.	
	22/10/17		Major HOBSON M.C. returning from leave assumed command of the Battalion.	
VAUGHAN'S BANK	23/10/17		Relieved by 15 Bn Cheshire Regt. Without incident. Moved back into Brigade Support – VAUGHANS BANK – W. WILLOWS – HEATH – LIMERICK and HOLME POSTS.	
	24/10/17 25/10/17		Rest and Carried Working Parties – Line very quiet.	

Army Form C. 2118.

WAR DIARY
or
INTELLIGENCE SUMMARY. 13TH (SERVICE) BATTN CHESHIRE REGT.

September

(Erase heading not required.)

Place	Date	Hour	Summary of Events and Information	Remarks and references to Appendices
VAUGHANS BANK.	25/9/17		Reconnoitred - BIRDCAGE - BUCKTHORN- HEYTHROP POSTS and RIFLE BANK. preparatory to relief :— Relief completed 10 P.M. without incident. 26/9/17	
THE NEST.	26/9/17		Line quiet	
	29/9/17		Officers of 1/5. Kings Own Royal Lancaster Regiment - 55th Division - reconnoitred our positions to relief.	
	29/9/17		Preparations for relief	
	30/9/17		Relief carried out without incident to 10.30 p.m. Battalion proceeded to camps at AIZECOURT le BAS.	

[signature]
Major
Commanding 13TH (SERVICE) BATTN CHESHIRE REGT.

WAR DIARY
or
INTELLIGENCE SUMMARY
(Erase heading not required.)

Army Form C. 2118.

10th Bn. The Cheshire Regiment
October 1917.

Vol 21

Place	Date	Hour	Summary of Events and Information	Remarks and references to Appendices
AIZECOURT	1/10/17		Battalion proceeded by Motor Lorry to PERONNE	
PERONNE	2/10/17		Billets in PERONNE - Inspection of two Officers and draft by Brigadier General - distribution of draft to companies - 2nd Lieut JACKSON joined the Battalion	
	3/10/17		Proceeded by train to ARRAS - Marched to rest at WANQUETIN - Settled in hutments 11 pm	
WANQUETIN	4/10/17		Training - Musketry - Bayonet. Lt Col ... - Bomb fighting & 3/7 Section by Brigadier	
	5/10/17		General at WARLUS 3/7 Section to Gun Guard at WARLUS - 2nd Lieut. ELLIOT	
	6/10/17		LOVE and ABLETT joined the Battalion	
	7/10/17		Entered - Section in Musketry by Major SOMERVILLE - Event of HORNS	
	8/10/17		Musketry under Staff Sergeant Instructions endorsed by Major SOMERVILLE	
	9/10/17		Training continued	
	10/10/17		Training continued - Lt Col B C Lord returned from leave - Event of HORNS	
	11/10/17		Training continued - Advance party left for billeting duty at ANNEKE	
	12/10/17		Training continued to ARRAS STATION - Entrained and proceeded at 4.45 am Party to CASSEL - Marched by night to ANNEKE - Settled in billets at 3 pm	
ANNEKE	13/10/17		Marched from CASSEL to ANNEKE	
	14/10/17		Resting in billets at ANNEKE	
ROVEN	15/10/17		Train to ROVEN - Camp outside ROVEN	
EVERDINGHE	16/10/17		Train to EVERDINGHE - Caused DUNWICH Camp and settled down 3 pm	
	17/10/17		Battn of HOULTHURST FOREST - inspections & renewal of falling kit	

Army Form C. 2118.

WAR DIARY
or
INTELLIGENCE SUMMARY.
(Erase heading not required.)

Instructions regarding War Diaries and Intelligence Summaries are contained in F. S. Regs., Part II. and the Staff Manual respectively. Title pages will be prepared in manuscript.

Place	Date	Hour	Summary of Events and Information	Remarks and references to Appendices
ELVERDINGHE	19/20/10/17		Took over front line South of HOUTHURST FOREST from 106 Infantry Brigade. X Co. in front line — W Co. (support) NORTHMOAL Fm. Z Co. (support) WIDTENDRIFT. Y Co. (support) GRUYTENSZAELE Fm.	
SOUTH OF HOUTHURST FOREST	21/22/10/17		Rest of 21/22 moved up into position for the attack - Point known as Albert carried out on morning of 22nd.	
	22/10/17		Reference Map Sheet 20 S.W. 4 1/10000. Position of Battalion at 5 p.m. 21st October 1917. H.Q. at VEE BEND. X Co. Holding front line from U 6 d 10.90 to U 6 d 25.75. W Co. in Shelters in U 15 d. Y Co. in Shell holes 200ᵗ S.E. of GRUYTENSZAELE Fm. Z Co. in Shelters at WIDTENDRIFT and near MONTMIRAIL Fm. Move to position of Assembly. The Battalion started to move into position at 5.30 pm 21/10/17. Y Co. went via VEE BEND, EGYPT HOUSE and LES 5 CHEMINS and were followed by Headquarters Signallers and Runners. W and Z Cos moved up along BURGES STREET and North of SUEZ Fm. - Casualties so under were sustained whilst moving up to Assembly - Y Co. 1 Officer 12 O.R. W " 1 " Z " 6 " Bn HQ	

WAR DIARY
or
INTELLIGENCE SUMMARY.
(Erase heading not required.)

Army Form C. 2118.

Place	Date	Hour	Summary of Events and Information	Remarks and references to Appendices
SOUTH OF HOUTHORST FOREST	22/10/17		**Forming up.** The operation of forming up so as laid down in B.O.O. No 51 was carried out satisfactorily and quietly and was concluded by 9.36 a.m. The arrangements made by Captain M.R. MAKIN — O.C. X Coy — for starting out to frontages as pointed out to him the previous Evening and for meeting the other companies sub guides worked most satisfactorily. The night was bitterly cold and there were heavy showers of hail, the rain increasing. Some discomfort and even wet though and provided both cold before zero hour arrived — the tea and rum provided by the Brigade did not reach VEE BEND — The Enemy kept a steady barrage of varying intensity N.E. and E along the line S. CHEMINS — LOUVOIS Fm. throughout the night. The barrage was not intense at 12 midnight and 2 a.m. and from 4 a.m. onwards. About 5 a.m. it reduced continuous and lost in the area of our front line and position of assembly and casualties occurred. **The Attack.** The Battalion advanced at Zero hour against the objective following our barrage closely. Though the barrage only went forward at the rate of 100 x Every 8 minutes, owing to the state of the ground which was a mass of shell holes containing at least a foot of water the troops needed the	

Army Form C. 2118.

WAR DIARY
or
INTELLIGENCE SUMMARY.
(Erase heading not required.)

Place	Date	Hour	Summary of Events and Information	Remarks and references to Appendices
SOUTH of HOULTHURST FOREST	22/10/17		almost effort and experienced the greatest difficulty in keeping up with the barrage. At 6.20 A.M. Y. Coy. 15 Bn. SHERWOODS began to arrive to hold our original front line and about the same time some slightly wounded men passed Bn. H.Q. but about 20 BUONORO and gave information that the attack was proceeding satisfactorily. At 6.50 A.M. Captain BURNETT came to Bn. H.Q. and reported that Y. Coy had gained their objective MARECHAL Fm. and BRUNETS and were consolidating; but that the centre and left were held up about V6a.5.5, that most of the rifles were useless owing to mud and that the losses were very heavy. Lt. Col. Dent arranged with Major MORTON commanding 15 Bn SHERWOODS for his Y. Coy. to hold up from our old front line towards V6a.5.5. and for him to hold our original front line. Lt. Col. Dent then sent forward with Captain BURNETT to V6a.5.5. collecting some stragglers in route and at the S.E. edge of wood (V6a.55.55. from there, Sentries were organised to try to outflank enemy pill box at V6a.55.70. which the enemy eventually evacuated; but any further advance was held up by rifle fire from trenches immediately north and from a pill box at V6a.40.95.	

WAR DIARY
INTELLIGENCE SUMMARY

Army Form C. 2118.

Place	Date	Hour	Summary of Events and Information	Remarks and references to Appendices
Outskirts of HOULTHURST FOREST	22/10/17		Lieut G Dent then went to COMBO House F. there to see Capt Willington M.C. O.C. Z Coy and shot School of the Machine Gun Coy. He had got a Lewis gun up to that point, all that remained of COMBO F. too a Lewis pill-box. When exploring the point Lt G had killed a German and gained a machine gun. Lt G 16th Ln R Scots Coy were consolidating about 50yds in front of COMBO House. Captain Willington pointed out his dispositions at MARECHAL Ft and informed Lt Col Dent that he had reduced to two platoons – he was then doubtful of N Coy – seeing it about two platoons and a message too sent to O.C. 15th Bn Sherwoods to have his M.G. from our original front line to COMBO House. – Lieut Sherwood M.G.C. was ordered to send a Vickers Gun to MARECHAL Ft. which was done, but too of the men taking it up were hit by Snipers and the barrel casing of the gun was punctured by a bullet. When leaving from the Assistant Adjutant of 15th L. R Scots Regt were being sent up Lieut Col Dent returned to Battn H.Q. about 11.30 a.m. At 1 p.m. V Coy 15th Cheshire took over our original front line. Captain and Adjutant GORDON POYFER went forward to obtain at about 1 p.m. and returned about 2.30 p.m. reporting that remnants of W.X. and V Coys were still up there and consolidating on the line U6a.6.6–U6a2.7.	

WAR DIARY or INTELLIGENCE SUMMARY

Army Form C. 2118.

Place	Date	Hour	Summary of Events and Information	Remarks and references to Appendices
SOUTH OF HOULTHURST FOREST	22/10/17		and were in touch with 14th Chaseurs on our left. The bn sent to the right and saw Captain Millington at COLOMBO HOUSE. The situation remained unchanged till about 4.30pm, when the enemy counter-attacked the left flank about V.6.a.3.9. in force force and under cover of an intense barrage and broke through. Sundry stragglers fired on from these oats the remnants of W.Y.Y. C/o 16th Chaseurs and 1 Coy 15 Shenwoods fell back out of the wood and took up a position for some time about V.6.a.6.4. but eventually fell back to our own line. The withdrawal of the flank allowed the enemy to bring transverse H.Gs fire on the left of Captain Millington's command holding MARECHAL Fm and his left withdrew to COLOMBO HOUSE - MARECHAL Fm road and faced WEST. — On being taken HILLINGTON'S left fell back the 17th Lancers two on our right fell back to line of road and Captain Millington seen to north of them were today to be withdraws them to COLOMBO HOUSE Fm. The position at 7.30pm was as above, the Chaseurs having refused their right flank to keep touch with us.	

WAR DIARY or INTELLIGENCE SUMMARY.

Army Form C. 2118.

Place	Date	Hour	Summary of Events and Information	Remarks and references to Appendices
SOUTH OF HOULTHURST FOREST	22/8/17		Our relief by 15th Cheshire Regt. started soon after midnight. X Coy of that Battalion taking over COLOMBO HOUSE and forming up on the V. Coy right of our original front line. — W Coy – 15 Cheshires were to prolong to the left on our original front line and connect with the Gloster. No news was received during the night that they had done so though it was assumed about a half of fact they had. Consequently during the light it was arranged about our left and at about 3 P.M. & A.M. on 23rd and announcing from the nature and density of the Enemy barrage and from the fire of our own guns that the Enemy were attacking, the O.C. 17 Batt who was asked to have two of his companies up to line EGYPT HOUSE – BEZ F5 – did so did, but our Artillery and 15 Cheshire rifle fire stopped the attack. About 9 P.M. – Col Cobran had arrived from LOUVOIS Fm and be learnt that W Coy 15 Cheshires had been in position some time on the left of our original front line – Col Cobran being Satisfied with the position about O.C Bart handed over about 10 A.M. 22/8/17 and left with the Adjutant – Casualties 9 Officers 337 other ranks.	

Army Form C. 2118.

WAR DIARY
or
INTELLIGENCE SUMMARY.
(Erase heading not required)

Instructions regarding War Diaries and Intelligence Summaries are contained in F. S. Regs., Part II. and the Staff Manual respectively. Title pages will be prepared in manuscript.

Place	Date	Hour	Summary of Events and Information	Remarks and references to Appendices
SOUTH OF HOLTHURST FOREST	23/10/17		The Battalion was relieved in the early hours by 15th Ch. Gds. Regt. and proceeded to WIZERN DROP. – About 9 am the they tuned to WOOD 15. When the brigade supplied Cocoa &c. – At 1 pm the Battalion marched to BOESINGHE and proceeded to ELVERDINGHE by train and from there marched to ENNIS CAMP.	
ELVERDINGHE	24/10/17 to 28/10/17		Resting and Reorganising at ENNIE CAMP. – Enemy Aeroplane bombed inflicted casualties on SHERWOODS in next camp.	
	29/10/17		Bat. left ENNIE CAMP about 3 pm and proceeded to COLDSTREAM CAMP (near canal) and settled into camp by 6 pm – The Battalion was Reserve to the Brigade and provided working parties for freezing Salteo at HOEKNIT. 7 camps shelled and bombed – no casualties	
COLDSTREAM CAMP	30/10/17		Work on Salteo continued	
	31/10/17		Work on Salteo continued	

B. C. Dent.
Lieut Colonel
Commanding 16th Bn. Ld. Ch Gds Regt.

WAR DIARY or INTELLIGENCE SUMMARY

Army Form C. 2118.

November   16th CHESHIRE REGT.   Vol 22

Place	Date	Hour	Summary of Events and Information	Remarks and references to Appendices
COLSTORM CAMP.	1/11/17		Upon relief by 11th Bn West Yorks the Battalion proceeded to DE WIPPE Camp	
DE WIPPE	2/11/17		Relief completed without incident and Battalion reached De Wippe at about 4 p.m.	
	3/11/17		Some spent on cleaning up and resting — Following reinforcements arrived 2 Subs — CAPT., 4 Lieut:- FLETCHER, CONSTANTINE, and 336 other ranks	
	4/11/17		Sandbagging huts and tents	
	5/11/17		Sandbagging huts and tents continued	
PROVEN.	6/11/17		Located to PROVEN by train — Entrained CROMBK 2pm. Marched into PERGOUT Camp located at 4.30pm — Everyone under canvas; but ground fairly hard and dry	
	7/11/17		Brigade inspected by Divisional Commander at 12 noon — Officers and for Camp improvements	
EVERDINGHE	8/11/17		Work on Camp continued	
	9/11/17		Marched to EVERDINGHE — reaching BLUNGTON Camp at 3 pm. It took us tramway — 150 other ranks taking camp on colo tramways — Remainder of Battalion marching and reaching here 10/11/17 Colnel Sant proceeded to a	
	10/11/17		Course returning on 14/11/17 Following reinforcements arrived 9/11/17 2nd Lieut. 7 Lt MURPHY and 6 O.R.s	
	15/11/17		Lts 14/11/17 2nd Lieut. at 46 O.R. Lts 14/11/17 2nd Lieut GROHL 90 other ranks	
	16/11/17		Work on tramways taken over by 17 Bn West Yorks — Battalion moved into BARKE Camp	
BARKE CAMP	17/11/17		Company training commenced at Mulhoy Wodo. Genl AYRES C in C and 1st Lieut Rivals TITTERTON Private MARSHALL. Rivals WALKER.	
	18/11/17		Divisional Commander presented Military Medals to	

HUDSON and BAND

WAR DIARY or INTELLIGENCE SUMMARY

Army Form C. 2118.

November 10th/S Bn Cheshire Regt.

Place	Date	Hour	Summary of Events and Information	Remarks and references to Appendices
BRAKE CAMP	19/11/17		Training continued	
	20/11/17		Training continued – Col. Dent proceeded to take over command of 104 Infantry Brigade for one month	
	21/11/17		Training continued – Notification received of following awards – Military Cross to Captain F.N. STEWART RAMC, Captain DONOVAN BURNETT, Lieut GALLAGHER. Distinguished Conduct Medal to 57860 Private JOHNSON W.A.	
	22/11/17		Training continued	
	23/11/17		Divisional Commander presented medal above – Major HODSON committed to line	
	24/11/17		Marched to KEMPTON PARK, halted for dinner, proceeded up the line and relieved 20th Lancashire Regt – Disposition W- Batt Company & extra company Y. Left company & Support company PHEASANT TRENCH – Batt. HQ MORFOLK HOUSE Line reconnoitred – Lieut JOYCE P.D. wounded and several other ranks. Casualties – Colonel CALLUM and Company Commanders of 5th Norwood reconnoitred line	
BELLEVUE	25/11/17		Captain H.D. RYALLS DSO taken ill both Captain GORDON BAYLEY ill with Gasses & Lieut Cpt. the Adjutant left. Gordon BAYLEY proceeded to Cloob House and took over command of the Regt. Company	

WAR DIARY or INTELLIGENCE SUMMARY

Army Form C. 2118.

November

16th (S) Bn: Cheshire Regt.

Place	Date	Hour	Summary of Events and Information	Remarks and references to Appendices
BELGIQUE	26/11/17		Relieved by 15th Sherwoods. Relief involved - Relief complete by 8 pm. Battalion went into support at KEMPTON PARK.	
KEMPTON PARK	27/11/17		Quiet day - noting - Captain H D RYALLS D.P.O. to hospital. 2nd Lieut Howells took over command of W Coy.	
	28/11/17		Battalion moved during afternoon to TURCO FARM CAMP for Salvage work in Divisional front Area.	
	29/11/17		10 pm orders re Salvage work cancelled - Battalion at Siege Camp in Divisional Support.	
	30/11/17		Battalion joined rest of Brigade at 4.30 pm reaching camp at ____ Training carried out.	

M. W. Dean Major
Commanding 16 Bn. Cheshire Regt.

Army Form C. 2118

WAR DIARY
or
INTELLIGENCE SUMMARY
(Erase heading not required.)

Vol 23

21 K
1 sheet

16th Battⁿ Cheshire Regᵗ

War Diary ~ December, 1917.

Army Form C. 2118.

WAR DIARY
or
INTELLIGENCE SUMMARY.
December 1917

(Erase heading not required.)

Place	Date	Hour	Summary of Events and Information	Remarks and references to Appendices
SIEGE CAMP	1/12/17		Training carried out – C.S.M COULTER P-11056 awarded "Croix de Guerre".	
	2/12/17		– do – ⎫	
	3/12/17		– do – ⎬ whilst forming part of the Brigade in support.	
	4/12/17		– do – ⎪	
	5/12/17		– do – ⎭	
POELCAPELLE	6/12/17		Relieved 20th L.F. in POELCAPELLE Sector – Battn Headquarters in NORFOLK HOUSE. Disposition – W. Right Company, X. Centre Company, Z. Left Company, Y. Support Company in PHEASANT TRENCH.	
	7/12/17		During the night 6th-7th a small Boche patrol was observed on the Right. Several were killed and one O.R. taken prisoner.	
	8/12/17		Usual Artillery activity – we succeeded in getting hot stew up to the men in the advanced posts. Another small hostile party seen on our Right was dispersed and one wounded prisoner taken.	
	9/12/17		Relieved at dusk by the Queen Victoria's Rifles – 58th Division – sustained 5 O.R. casualties on the way out to SIEGE CAMP. The Battalion moved by train to LE NOUVEAU MONDE near HERZEELE.	

Cdg. 16TH (SERVICE) BATTn CHESHIRE REGT.

Army Form C. 2118.

WAR DIARY
INTELLIGENCE SUMMARY
(Erase heading not required.)

December 1917

Place	Date	Hour	Summary of Events and Information	Remarks and references to Appendices
LE NOUVEAU MONDE.	10/12/17		Resting and cleaning up. Meeting of Commanding Officers at 105th Infantry Brigade Headquarters to arrange a Brigade Assault-at-Arms.	
SCHOOL CAMP.	11/12/17		105th Infantry Brigade moved to SCHOOL CAMP near POPERINGHE	
	12/12/17		training and reorganisation.	
	13/12/17		— do —	
	14/12/17		Training continued - the following reinforcements reported for duty - CAPTAIN T. HADDON, LIEUT. O. STEAD, 2nd Lts G.H. GATES, F.G. NORRIS, T.F. PAUL-JONES. LIEUT-COL. B.C. DENT and 20600 Cpl. W.E. FREESTONE (W Coy) mentioned in dispatches - LONDON GAZETTE, Dec 14th 1917	
	15/12/17		Training continued	
	16/12/17		— do —	
	17/12/17		— do —	
	18/12/17		— do —	
	19/12/17		— do —	
	20/12/17		— do — 2nd LIEUT. PAUL JONES detailed for duty as CAMP ADJUTANT at LANGEMARCK (?)	
	21/12/17		Training. 2nd LIEUT E PANTER proceeded to ENGLAND on transfer to TANK-CORPS Lecture to all officers and N.C.O.s by an R.F.C. Officer	

Sgd. [signature]
Lt. Col. Comdg 13th Cheshire Regt.

Army Form C. 2118.

WAR DIARY
INTELLIGENCE SUMMARY
(Erase heading not required.)

December 1917.

Instructions regarding War Diaries and Intelligence Summaries are contained in F.S. Regs., Part II. and the Staff Manual respectively. Title pages will be prepared in manuscript.

Place	Date	Hour	Summary of Events and Information	Remarks and references to Appendices
SCHOOL CAMP	22/12/17		Training – III Corps Commander inspected and addressed all officers of 105th Inf. Bde.	
	23/12/17		105th Infantry Brigade Assault at Arms – we won Officers Revolver Shooting Competition	
	24/12/17		—do— No 9 Platoon, 16th Bn CHESHIRE REGT. won the Brigade Platoon Rapid Fire Compett; "Z" Coy. won the Brigade Bombing Compett: Church Parades: followed by Xmas Dinner for the men, the Dining Hall being suitably decorated for the occasion.	
	25/12/17		Brigade Competitions resumed – Rapid Fire Competition for the best Batt⁻ Team won by us – W. Coy. won the Brigade Lewis Gun Competition	
	26/12/17		Preliminary rounds of the Brigade Boxing Compett: Lt Col. B.C. DENT relinquished the temporary command of the 105th Inf. Bde. and proceeded to ENGLAND for duty with a Machine Gun Battalion	
	27/12/17		Finals of the Boxing Compett: we won five events out of the possible six. Distribution of Prizes by Brig. General MIRINDIN, commanding 105th Inf. Bde. We won 3 silver bugles out of 4 offered by the Brigade, and 10 events out of the possible 16 – several events postponed on account of the frost.	
	28/12/17		Training resumed.	
	29/12/17		Church Parades. 16th Bn CHESHIRE REGT. selected to represent the 105th Inf. Bde. in the Rapid Fire Compett: to be held under the auspices of the 35th Division	
	30/12/17			
	31/12/17		Training continued.	

MWMMahajn
Cdg
16th (SERVICE) BATT⁻ CHESHIRE REGT.

15th (SERVICE) BATT'N CHESHIRE REGT

Army Form C. 2118.

WAR DIARY
or
INTELLIGENCE SUMMARY.
(Erase heading not required.)

JANUARY 1918

Place	Date	Hour	Summary of Events and Information	Remarks and references to Appendices
SCHOOL CAMP POPERINGHE	1/1/18		Training Continued — rapid fire — platoon attack — E.S — Lewis in support.	
	2/1/18		do	
	3/1/18		do — Divisional Assault at Arms — Evelyn hood cup - Battalion won 2nd	
	4/1/18		do — Corporal Wright won 1st Weight Lifting	
	5/1/18		do	
	6/1/18		Church Parade	
	7/1/18		Training Continued	
	8/1/18		do	
	9/1/18		Left SCHOOL CAMP 6.30 PM Marched to PROVEN Station. Entrained 8.45 PM for ELVERDINGHE. Marched to BRIDGE CAMP and relieved 2/2 LONDON REGT — 58th Division	
BRIDGE CAMP ELVERDINGHE	10/1/18		Sacked Souters DIVISIONAL RESERVE	4 Drafts
	11/1/18		Training Continued — Constructed Rifle Range	
	12/1/18		do	
	13/1/18		Church Parade	
	14/1/18		Training Continued	

16th (SERVICE) BATTN CHESHIRE REGT.

Army Form C. 2118.

WAR DIARY
or
INTELLIGENCE SUMMARY.
(Erase heading not required.)

JANUARY 1918

Instructions regarding War Diaries and Intelligence Summaries are contained in F. S. Regs., Part II. and the Staff Manual respectively. Title pages will be prepared in manuscript.

Place	Date	Hour	Summary of Events and Information	Remarks and references to Appendices
BRIDGE CAMP				
EVERDINGHE	15/1/18		Training Continued	
KEMPTON PARK	16/1/18		Handed to KEMPTON PARK. Relieved 3rd Bn Lancashire Fus. as Right Support Battalion. Dispositions – X and Y Companies at KEMPTON PARK. W. and Z. at PHEASANT FARM Trench.	
	17/1/18		Burial service – CORPS LINE – POELCAPPELLE – BREWERY.	
	18/1/18		Inter Company Relief completed by 4.15pm without incident. Lieut J HARE evacuated to Hospital. MEASLES. Transport taken over by 2nd Lieut G.B.FOX.	
	19/1/18		Burial Service – CORPS LINE – POELCAPPELLE – BREWERY	
NORFOLK HOUSE POELCAPPELLE	20/1/18		Relieved 15th Ln Cheshire Regt in line – Bn HQ. NORFOLK HOUSE. W. Right (GLOSTER FARM) Z. Left (BREWERY) Y Centre B (POELCAPPELLE) X Support B (PHEASANT TRENCH) – Relief completed by 6.30 pm without incident. Work on posts and wiring continued.	
	21/1/18		Quiet day – Wiring and improvements continued.	
	22/1/18		Inter Company Relief completed without incident by 6.15 pm – Wiring reinforcement continued.	
	24/1/18		Relieved by 20th Lan Fus. Relief completed without incident by 6.35 pm. Proceeded to KEMPTON PARK.	
KEMPTON PARK	25/1/18		Resting and cleaning – Capt. F.W.BIGLAND, 2nd Lieut R.P. BUSH and 2nd Lieut G.P. COCKS arrived as reinforcements.	

WAR DIARY
or
INTELLIGENCE SUMMARY. JANUARY 1918

Army Form C. 2118.

16TH (SERVICE) BATTN CHESHIRE REGT.

Instructions regarding War Diaries and Intelligence Summaries are contained in F. S. Regs. Part II. and the Staff Manual respectively. Title pages will be prepared in manuscript.

(Erase heading not required.)

Place	Date	Hour	Summary of Events and Information	Remarks and references to Appendices
HEMPTON PARK	26/1/18		Resting - Cleaning - Training continued	
	27/1/18		do	
	28/1/18		do	
	29/1/18		Working parties 2 Officers 200 Oth. Ranks. Bath taken over by 15th Cheshire	
			Training continued	
	30/1/18		do	
	31/1/18		Working parties 1 Officer 95 Oth. Ranks. Training continued	

M. ??? Major
Commanding 16TH (SERVICE) BATTN CHESHIRE REGT.

WAR DIARY 10TH (SERVICE) BATT'N CHESHIRE REGT.
INTELLIGENCE SUMMARY

February

Vol 25

Place	Date	Hour	Summary of Events and Information	Remarks and references to Appendices
KEMPTON PARK	1/2/18		Quiet day - A.E. working parties continued - Preparatory measures for demobilising commenced	
	2/2/18		Captain Denton (wounded 22/11/17) rejoined the Battalion - Work as on 1st continued	
	3/2/18		Relieved as Right support Battalion by 1st Staffords, relief completed by 9 am without incident. Brigadier General inspected and spoke to draft of 5 officers and 100 other ranks who are to proceed to 1/6 Cheshire or 1st unit. Left Kempton Park and proceeded to BRIDGE JUNCTION Camp at 9.30 am, arriving there at 11.30 am. Draft of 15 officers and 310 other ranks transferred to 15th Cheshire at 2pm.	
BRIDGE JUNCTION	4/2/18		Sept of Officers and other ranks left POPERINGHE at 11.15 am by train to join 1/6 Cheshire. Surplus details - cleaning equipment &c.	
	5/2/18		Training and recreational training continued	
	6/2/18		Training continued	
	7/2/18		Court of Inquiry re Absence of Lewis handed in to 2nd J. Cole - 2nd J Clarke - President Capt Silvester	
	8/2/18		Entrained - Surplus details left WOESTEN by train at 10am to proceed to II Corps REINFORCEMENTS (SURPLUS Wing) at BOLLEZEELE - Crossed BOLLEZEELE at 2pm marched to MERCKEGHEM	
MERCKEGHEM			and handed over to MAJOR W. HANCOCK D.S.O. - O.C. Surplus Wing -	

WAR DIARY

16TH (SERVICE) BATTN CHESHIRE REGT.

INTELLIGENCE SUMMARY.

February

Place	Date	Hour	Summary of Events and Information	Remarks
	8/2/18		The following letters were received by the Commanding Officer – Major (Acting Lieut Colonel) B.W. HODSON M.C.	

From Brigadier General POLLARD C.M.G. (acting Divisional Commander)

" I am sure I am voicing General Shute's feelings in "
" writing to you to say how sorry I am that your gallant "
" Battalion is being broken up, and to sympathise with all "
" those brave people of all ranks who must so deeply feel "
" their old Battalion. But I hope Service will & ask "
" to carry on the old spirit in their new homes. "

From Brigadier General Marindin D.S.O. (105' Infantry Brigade Commander)

" It is hardly necessary for me to say how bitterly I regret "
" I dreed the breaking up of your Battalion. During the 2½ months I have "
" Commanded this Brigade, your Battalion has done consistently well and "
" has gone on getting better and better and more efficient, till finally "
" by its gallant conduct in the attack at MOEUVRES, it gained a "

Army Form C. 2118.

WAR DIARY
16TH (SERVICE BATTN) CHESHIRE REGT.
INTELLIGENCE SUMMARY.
February

(Erase heading not required.)

Instructions regarding War Diaries and Intelligence Summaries are contained in F. S. Regs., Part II. and the Staff Manual respectively. Title pages will be prepared in manuscript.

Place	Date	Hour	Summary of Events and Information	Remarks and references to Appendices
	8/2/18		" very high reputation as a fighting Battalion.	
			" The Brigade and the Battalion are at the very top of their	"
			" form and a strong 'esprit de corps' exists throughout the	"
			" Brigade. The loss of your Battalion will be felt keenly	"
			" throughout the Brigade and by none more so than myself.	"
			" I can only wish you and all ranks of your Battalion	"
			" the best of luck there – Ever you go and are absolutely	"
			" confident that where – Ever individuals may go, they will remember	"
			" the traditions of their old Battalion and its old Brigade.	"

[signature]
Actg Lieut Colonel
16TH (SERVICE BATTN) CHESHIRE REGT.

www.ingramcontent.com/pod-product-compliance
Lightning Source LLC
Chambersburg PA
CBHW081557160426
43191CB00011B/1955